50p   4/:

CW00602897

TREKKING IN THE
USA

AA

TREKKING IN THE
USA

Texts by
Fabio Penati and Vincenzo Martegani
Photographs by
Vincenzo Martegani

AA

Copyright © 1989 Arnoldo Mondadori Editore S.p.A., Milan
English translation copyright © 1990 Arnoldo Mondadori Editore
S.p.A. Milan

Translated by John Gilbert

Photographs are by Vincenzo Martegani except for those in the
Glacier National Park chapter, which are by Agenzia Speranza.

Distributed in the United Kingdom by the Publishing Division of The Automobile Association,
Fanum House, Basingstoke, Hampshire RG21 2EA.

This edition published 1990 by The Automobile Association,
Fanum House, Basingstoke, Hampshire RG21 2EA.

A CIP catalogue record for this book is available from the British
Library.

ISBN 0 7495 0036 0

Printed and bound in Italy by Arnoldo Mondadori Editore, Verona

CONTENTS

INTRODUCTION

The United States is a land of immense spaces and enormous distances, and the term "wilderness" can still be applied legitimately to some areas, despite the consequences of human action, whether deliberate or unintentional, which has reduced them drastically both in number and size.

Many of these areas, now protected and maintained with the specific aim of preserving the natural environment and its delicate equilibrium, as well as local culture and history, are unrivalled as tourist attractions. The national parks, monuments and reserves offer a boundless variety of walks and drives in natural settings of breathtaking grandeur and beauty. The visitor can roam the length and breadth of these vast stretches of unspoiled country in comfort and, thanks to the patrol services of the rangers, in virtually total safety.

How to use the guide

The main purpose of this guide is to offer the reader an easy and convenient means of choosing places to visit in the United States. The emphasis is on areas of particular interest to the first-time visitor and with this in mind we have tried to offer a cross-section of the many varied types of natural surroundings. First of all we need to indicate the type of information contained in the guide and, most importantly, where to find it.

This introductory section provides general information and advice about travel and accommodation in the United States, the protected areas, clothing and equipment, and indispensable reading matter.

The bulk of the book is divided into ten chapters, which describe individual areas of interest, arranged alphabetically by state. Each chapter is broken down into three parts – an information section, a main text and a series of boxed texts. The information includes important facts such as access routes, entry fees, roads, service stations, accommodation, etc. The main text broadly outlines the history of the area, sometimes illustrating natural features, and gives the individual itineraries, usually described as "trails," indicating distance, changes in elevation, time required, level of difficulty and elements of special interest. The boxes provide detailed information about campsites, known as campgrounds, climate, plants and animals, particular features of local landscape and/or wildlife, practical tips and advice on photography.

An index of place names is given at the end of the book.

Protected areas

The areas described in this guide form part of the extensive network of areas administered by the United States National Park Service. Eight are classified as national parks, one as a national monument and one as a scenic area, but these definitions involve no substantial differences.

Regulations

Each area has a specific code of regulations which dictates what visitors can and cannot do within the confines of the park; the code can vary from one area to another according to different environmental conditions and, where relevant, this is mentioned in the individual chapters, but the majority of rules apply everywhere.

In general it is forbidden to pick flowers, to kill animals (with or without firearms), to feed them, and to remove fossils, minerals, rock fragments or archaeological finds.

With rare exceptions, you are not allowed to light fires away from special cooking enclosures attached to campgrounds and picnic areas, and to make use of locally collected wood; anyone wishing to have a barbecue must buy wood or another fuel outside the park or, where available, from general stores inside the park. Campers are permitted to use gas for cooking.

Pitching a tent outside official campgrounds, which provide the only accommodation on longer treks because there are virtually no huts or shelters, is strictly controlled everywhere. Apart from various restrictions to be followed, such as a minimum distance to be left between tent and roads, footpaths and streams, areas that are prohibited, etc., it is necessary to obtain a Backcountry Permit which is issued free of charge by the rangers, in accordance with the number of people already out on the various trails.

Finally it is strictly forbidden to dump any kind of refuse; organic waste matter must be carefully buried, and anything else (paper, plastic, cans, glass, etc.) carried until you find a bin.

Golden Eagle Passport

The Golden Eagle Passport is a card, valid for one year, that allows access to all parks, monuments, zones of historic interest and recreation areas administered by the National Park Service free of charge.

The card, which can be bought at the entrance to any of the above-mentioned protected areas, confers the right of free entry to the holder and all passengers of their vehicle (car, truck camper, motorcycle, etc.). When entry is by public transport or some other means (on foot, bicycle, etc.), the right of entry extends to the card-holder's family. It is non-transferable and is issued annually to run from 1 January to 31 December, valid for an unlimited number of visits. At present it costs $25, and bearing in mind that the average entry fee is $5, it represents a considerable saving for the visitor.

Further information

The protected areas of the National Park System are each individually administered by a team of staff led by a superintendent. For each area mentioned in the guide the superintendent's address and telephone number are given; and requests in writing or by phone will bring information and illustrated material by return through the mail, free of charge.

There are also many publications available on general and specific subjects. Among the best are Michael Frome's fine book, *National Park Guide*, published by Rand McNally, which describes all the areas in the National Park System and, quite indispensable, *The Complete Guide to America's National Parks*, published every two years by the National Park Foundation, which provides up-to-date practical information (charges, where to eat and sleep, activities, climatic charts, etc.).

More detailed and of greater interest to the naturalist are the four splendid volumes of the series entitled *The Sierra Club Guides to the National Parks*, published by the Sierra Club, one of the oldest and most renowned environmental associations in the United States, and available in major international libraries. In addition there are many books, including interesting tourist guides, published by local naturalist groups, available either on the spot or by mail. Requests for catalogues and prices can be made by writing directly to the associations concerned (the addresses are given in each chapter) or to the superintendent. For the nature-lover, in addition to the books already mentioned, there are numerous guides available on the recognition of trees, flowers, amphibians and reptiles, birds and mammals, costing around $10–15, which make it fairly easy to identify at least the most common plants and animals likely to be encountered along the way. Particularly recommended are those published by the National Audubon Society and the *Peterson Field Guides* which fit neatly into a rucksack.

Clothing and equipment

The areas described in this guide represent a range of highly varied situations which cannot be discussed individually. In general it is worth remembering that for walking in desert zones lightweight garments, which nevertheless do not leave too much skin uncovered, are advisable by day, both to avoid excessive perspiration (loss of water and salts) and the risk of burning. Something warm to wear during the cooler nights should also be included. When preparing for mountain walking, remember that the weather and temperature can change rapidly in these areas so you will need to pack clothing to combat the possible cold and damp as well as lighter layers to avoid burning from the strong sunshine. A hat and sunglasses are essential for both mountain and desert walking.

Shoes, like everything else, must be suitable for the type of ground to be covered. Apart from special requirements such as footwear for climbing, normal walking shoes are generally the most comfortable. It is best to choose a pair that is lightweight and with a flexible sole for walking on flat surfaces and much used paths, and a stronger pair (but never one with a hard sole) for rocky, stony or difficult ground. Moreover it is advisable to avoid walking shoes with warm linings for tackling desert terrain because the feet will become far too hot and uncomfortable.

If a long journey is intended, adequate camping equipment is very important. This should include a gas stove or water heater (if only to make a cup of tea) and a container for drinking water, of which there is little or none at all in desert zones and in the Everglades. A compass and altimeter are only indispensable when tackling "off-trails," i.e. those away from signposted paths, in combination with detailed maps which can be bought on the spot.

Finally, do not forget when packing your rucksack to leave room for all your camera equipment (see the photographic advice given in each chapter) and a pair of binoculars. The scenery you will enjoy will more than compensate for their weight on your shoulders.

Degrees of difficulty

Every itinerary in this guide is classified according to its relative degree of difficulty. Authors adopt various methods of assessment but for the present purposes we have made three simple subdivisions:

E = Easy
M = Moderate
D = Demanding

These three initial letters convey an overall assessment of the itinerary in question, taking into consideration the following factors:
– type of route (road, path, track, trail, etc.), terrain (wood, grassland, stony ground, etc.) and surface (smooth, broken, etc.).
– whether or not signposted (direction posts, painted signs, piles of stones, etc.).
– change in elevation, length of route, steepness of ascent and duration of walk.
– possible difficulties of orientation or traceability.
– maximum height, steepness of slopes, clear marking of path.
– other variants (lack of water, accessibility, etc.).

More specifically, the letters may be defined as follows:

E = Easy. Itineraries with clearly marked routes (thanks to signposting and/or positioning of the paths themselves) and therefore not posing any uncertainties, difficulties or problems of orientation; with only a few exceptions, these normally occur at under 2,000 m (6,500 ft), entail at most a 200–300 m (650–1,000 ft) change in elevation, and involve not much more than 3 hours' walking.

M = Moderate. Itineraries that are generally confined to signposted paths, occasionally along trails, with changes in elevation that are somewhat greater than those in the previous category. The walks may be long and fairly tiring but they can all be done in one or at most two days. It is essential to be in good physical condition before undertaking these.

D = Demanding. Long treks of several days along marked or unmarked paths and tracks, which may require the ability to determine direction by means of maps and compass, crossing varied and uncommon types of terrain, though not presenting any mountaineering problems. These routes demand excellent mental and physical preparation, which is best attainable by first attempting a few preliminary "training" hikes.

Practical information

Visitors to the United States travelling on EEC passports no longer require a visa provided they are staying no longer than 90 days. No vaccinations are required, except for those travelling from zones where infection is present. An international driving license is not necessary.

General suggestions

Early booking of flights and car rental is advisable in order to obtain your desired departure and arrival dates and to take advantage of competitive fares, particularly if you wish to travel during the summer months. Remember to reconfirm your return flight at least seventy-two hours before scheduled departure.

In the United States medical treatment is very expensive, so it is a good idea to arrange private medical insurance beforehand.

For electrical appliances, the current is

110–115 volt/60 cycle AC and sockets are different from European types. You can telephone abroad from virtually any telephone box. It is possible to reverse the charges by dialling 0 and asking for a "collect call."

How to travel

The United States is the ideal country for long-distance travel. An extensive network of highways (free of charge), efficient public services and countless motels providing every level of comfort make it possible to journey the length and breadth of the land without risk of problems.

Air travel is second to none, given the size of the country, for major journeys, either from coast to coast or from the center in either direction. Internal flights are numerous and cheap. The special ticket VISIT U.S.A., available to travellers not resident in the United States, can be bought beforehand to cover three flights, only one of which need be booked at the time. If you do not want to be tied down by prior booking and wish to enjoy greater freedom of choice, and provided you have the time and patience, you can put yourself on standby and almost always get a flight within a few hours. Ground facilities and services are as a rule excellent, and there are frequent connecting flights between cities.

A car is the best and most economical means for travelling about as you please, particularly for four people. The vehicles have a high standard of comfort and are cheap to run with air conditioning, automatic drive, the ridiculously low cost of gasoline and toll-free highways. Europeans have to adjust to a lower speed limit, which is strictly enforced, than they are used to but considering the volume of traffic on American roads good average speeds can be maintained. Remember, too, that the legal alcohol limit in the U.S.A. is the equivalent of one double whisky or three beers.

Cars may be hired from any of the big companies, but by using smaller firms or local garages it is possible to make a saving of around 20 per cent. It is important to decide, before signing the car rental agreement, whether you are going to return it to the same place or to a different town, and to make sure that insurance is included in the price. Rental of the car requires the payment of a fairly high deposit, but this can be avoided by presenting a credit card – a method of payment which in any event is invaluable in the U.S.A.

Road maps are extremely detailed and well produced, particularly those published by Rand McNally, available in bookstores and at gas stations.

Trailers (caravans) and truck campers (caravan campers) are becoming ever more popular but require prior booking, which may prove restricting. They are slower and less easy to manage than a car and will be more expensive. Although unsuitable for visiting cities, they are extremely useful for touring parks and for travelling through small towns.

The bus is the cheapest form of transport for those on their own who are unable to share the cost of travelling by car with others.

Where to eat

Breakfast in the States is usually a filling meal which will satisfy the most demanding appetite and carry the visitor through until evening. At midday it need only be supplemented by a snack, which is certainly the most practical solution for anyone engaged in travelling and not wishing to waste time during the course of the day. Dinner in the evening can then be enjoyed in a relaxed frame of mind. In the big cities there is an enormous choice, ranging from full meals in a large restaurant (many of them offering specialized national cuisine) to more modest fare in one of the ubiquitous fast-food establishments such as McDonald's or Burger King, with, of course, every other

possibility in between. Out of town the choice is somewhat more limited but seldom poses any problems. The best solution for the visitor is to frequent smaller restaurants serving fixed menus where the quality of food is usually excellent and rather more imaginative than that of the large chains. Beers are very good indeed, rather lighter than those in Europe, and so are the wines, usually Californian, which tend to be medium-sweet.

Where to stay

Americans are always on the move and so, wherever you go, you are bound to find ample accommodation facilities which are comfortable and efficiently run. Particularly popular and convenient are the motels (far removed from the establishments that go by that name in Europe) which are often provided with swimming-pools and other recreational facilities.

There are chains of first-class luxury motels as well as much cheaper ones; obviously they vary in comfort according to price. Finding a room is fairly easy but it is best to start looking around early in the afternoon. At weekends it is advisable to book beforehand and this can be done free of charge from any hotel of the same chain on the morning prior to departure.

There are numerous campgrounds throughout the United States, and this form of accommodation is especially recommended inside the national parks and in the immediate neighbourhood. It is a good idea to acquaint yourself each time with the regulations of the site.

The prices for accommodation given in this guide were correct at the time of going to press but inevitably some variation may occur. The main purpose of their inclusion is to provide a guideline for travellers to help in the calculation of their budget.

GRAND CANYON

NATIONAL PARK

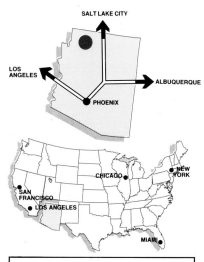

Address: Superintendent, Grand Canyon National Park, PO Box 129, Grand Canyon, Arizona 86023, tel. (602) 638-7888.
Area: Over 3,000 km² (1,160 sq. miles).
Altitude: 370–2,800 m (1,200–9,000 ft) above sea level.
Access: The park is divided into two sectors, to the south and north of the Colorado River The South Rim is reached by State Highway 64, the North Rim by State Highway 67.
Opening times: The South Rim is open all year round, the North Rim from mid May to end October.
Entry charge: $5 per car; Golden Eagle Passport valid.
Parking: At viewpoints, Visitor Center.

A few statistics will suffice to give some idea of the size of the Grand Canyon cut out by the Colorado River: depth 1,600 m (5,250 ft), width between 180 m and 30 km (600 ft and 19 miles), length 443 km (277 miles). The National Park was set up in order to preserve the canyon, the river and the adjoining territory. Unfortunately, however, it has not prevented human technology from altering the hydro-geological equilibrium of the Colorado. In fact, the construction of the Glen Canyon dam, which by harnessing the water upriver of the park created the immense artificial basin of Lake Powell, not only altered the river's rate of flow but also caused a marked drop in its temperature. The consequence of this has been a change among the fish population, favouring certain species at the expense of others which have virtually disappeared. However, this is only the last chapter in the story of the Grand Canyon.

Four thousand years of mankind

Fifty years ago a group of archaeologists excavating a cave in the Grand Canyon discovered some carved wooden statuettes, probably depicting animals, dating back to at least 2000 B.C. This find revolutionized the thinking of scientists who had always believed the first inhabitants of the region to have been the Anasazi, who reached the area around A.D. 500. These people, unlike the ancient Indians responsible for the statuettes, of whom almost nothing is known, were certainly hunters and farmers. In about A.D. 700 the Cohonina Indians also penetrated the region, but,

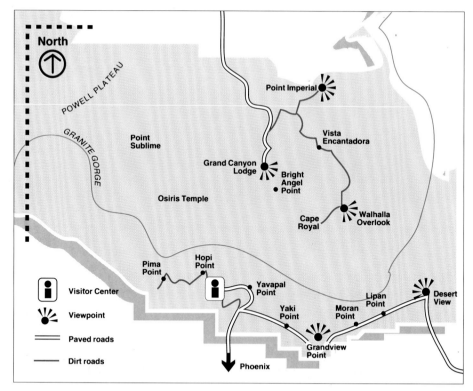

Fuel: There are two service stations in the South Rim (Visitor Center and Desert View) and one in the North Rim; others are situated along the access roads.

Roads: In addition to State Highways 64 and 67, West Rim Drive and East Rim Drive in the South Rim are paved, and these lead to Cape Royal and Point Imperial in the North Rim, where there is also an unpaved road, impassable after rain, leading to Point Sublime.

Shops: At Grand Canyon Village, at Desert View (South Rim) and at North Rim.

Accommodation: Grand Canyon Village (South Rim) has motels, hotels and cabins open all year round; book well in advance through Reservations Dept., Grand Canyon National Park Lodges, Grand Canyon, AZ 86023. Grand Canyon Lodge (North Rim) is open only from mid May to end October; for information contact TW Services Inc., 451 North Main, Cedar City, Utah 84720, tel. (801) 586-7686.

Visitor Center: This is in Grand Canyon Village and provides information, maps, books and exhibitions. In the North Rim sector the Ranger Station at the entrance performs a similar function and Grand Canyon Lodge provides information only.

Museums: The Yavapai Museum near the Visitor Center illustrates the geological history of the Grand Canyon, while the Tusayan Museum, along East Rim Drive near Desert View, specializes in archaeology.

Viewpoints: These are numerous in both sectors and mostly accessible by car.

Guided tours: Detailed programmes are available from the information centers.

Other activities: Mule rides last-

ing one or two days must be booked well in advance during the summer by writing, for the South Rim, to Reservations Dept., Grand Canyon National Park Lodges, Grand Canyon, AZ 86023, or for the North Rim to Grand Canyon Trail Rides, Box 1638, Cedar City, UT 84720. Horse rides can also be arranged. In addition, private tour operators organize trips down the Colorado River by motorboat or raft, lasting a maximum of three weeks (see list of names at the Visitor Center).

It is also possible to go trekking with a professional guide in the North Rim sector (enquire at Visitor Center).

Facilities for the disabled: Easy access to most public buildings; special brochures are available, and the option of raising any specific requirements when you make a booking.

like the Anasazi, they abandoned it around 1150 because of a long period of drought. Some 150 years later the Cerbat, considered to be the ancestors of the Hualapai and the Havasupai, two tribes who still live in the reserves south of the park, migrated to the South Rim area; and at the same time the ancestors of the present-day Paiute settled in the forests of the North Rim.

The first whites to see the Grand Canyon were the Spaniards attached to the Cardenas expedition of 1540 who spent some three days trying to find a passage for the descent of the river. The canyon was rediscovered in 1776 by a Spanish priest named Francisco Tomas Garcés who remained for some time with the Havasupai. However, reliable reports of the first Americans go back only to 1826: a fur trapper named James Ohio Pattie referred in his diary to the awesome mountains of the Grand Canyon, and it is clear he was by no means enamoured of the place. Equally negative was the judgement of an army lieutenant who was sent in 1857 to lead an expedition with the aim of charting the Colorado River region. He wrote in his report: "The region is surely without any value. Ours was the first, and undoubtedly the last, group of whites to visit these places from which it is impossible to extract any profit." Such an opinion raises a smile today but it should not be forgotten that a profound change in thinking had to come about before it was recognized that the natural heritage itself was of value and needed to be conserved. Towards the end of the century the first tourist path, the Bright Angel Trail, was marked out, while the Santa Fé Railroad constructed a track to bring trains as close as possible to the canyon (this track can still be seen in Grand Canyon Village).

It was a group of former mining prospectors who first sensed the potential attraction of the area to the growing tourist trade, and soon the first hotels went up. In 1908 President Roosevelt declared the Grand Canyon a national monument, and only eleven years later, on 26 February 1919, it was transformed into a National Park.

The present boundaries are not those of the original park, for in 1975 the area was almost doubled to comprise the entire canyon proper from the confluence of the Paria River to Lake Mead, except for a few tracts included in the Indian reserves.

CLIMATE

The park's climate is extremely varied. The western end of the canyon floor lies at an altitude of 370 m (1,200 ft) while some of the North Rim peaks rise to 2,800 m (9,000 ft); and between these levels there are four or five distinct climatic belts. These zones succeed one another vertically and comprise every type of climate likely to be encountered when crossing the North American continent from north to south.

The lowest zone, lying between the bottom of the canyon and about 750 m (2,500 ft), is called the Lower Sonoran and is characterized by a hot, dry desert climate: the mean summer temperature is around 40°C (104°F) and there is little more than 250 mm (10 in) of rainfall per year. Between 750 m (2,500 ft) and 1,800 m (6,000 ft) is the Upper Sonoran zone, with high desert climatic conditions, similar to those of Capitol Reef and the Arches. Above 1,800 m (6,000 ft) is the so-called Transition zone, with a fairly mild mean summer temperature, little more than 20°C (68°F), and higher precipitation (average annual rainfall 355 mm [14 in]) which during the winter may fall as snow (average 155 cm [5 ft]). This is the climate of Grand Canyon Village at 2,091 m (6,373 ft) and of the South Rim. The climate of the North Rim, which is about 300 m (1,000 ft) higher, and thus situated in the so-called Canadian zone extending from 2,400 m (7,000 ft) to 2,700 m (9,000 ft), is different; here it is colder, with higher precipitation: rainfall exceeds 700 mm (27 in) a year, mostly occurring in the form of summer storms, while snowfall may be as much as 250 cm (12 ft), necessitating the closure of the North Rim from end October to mid May.

The ideal climatic conditions for walkers in the South Rim sector and inside the canyon are in spring and fall; the best time for visiting the North Rim is summer and September to mid October, particularly in autumn for the fall colours.

USEFUL ADVICE

The Grand Canyon is one of the busiest American parks. It is advisable, therefore, to avoid visiting the South Rim in July and August when the number of tourists not only creates considerable advance booking problems but also prevents full appreciation of the beauty spots.

On the other hand, the winter period affords a more leisurely holiday, including the more rewarding pursuits such as guided trips, mule rides, treks of several days, etc.

There are never problems of overcrowding in the North Rim sector.

Given the immense size of the park, it is as well to plan your journey in advance, bearing in mind that, although the distance from the South Rim to the North Rim is only 16 km (10 miles) as the crow flies, it is over 340 km (212 miles), or five hours' driving to get from one side of the Colorado River to the other. This is no problem, of course, for hikers, who can simply cross the river by two small, narrow suspension bridges, just wide enough to take a mule (see Bright Angel Trail and South Kaibab Trail).

Because of the enormous number of tourists, numbers allowed on trails which involve several days' hiking is suitably regulated to avoid eventual damage to the ecology of the area.

The Backcountry Reservations Offices, one at South Rim and the other at North Rim, issue the necessary Backcountry Use Permits either on the spot or booked beforehand through the mail. If you are writing before departure, applications should reach these offices not before 1 October of the year preceding the planned visit (e.g. not before 1 October 1990 for spring 1991).

The offices promptly mail back all necessary material for choosing itineraries and for tackling the trails (map, description of the area, regulations, etc.) and application forms, if requested (Backcountry Reservations Office, Grand Canyon National Park, PO Box 129, Grand Canyon, Arizona 86023, tel. (602) 638-2474). In addition, highly detailed guides are published by the Grand Canyon Natural History Association and may be bought by mail even from abroad; a catalogue of the guides is obtainable by applying directly to the Grand Canyon Natural History Association, PO Box 399, Grand Canyon, Arizona 86023, tel. (602) 638-7774.

Finally, it is advisable to prepare yourselves to have along on your hikes at least 3–5 pints (2 liters) of water per person per day, especially for long treks in summer.

Two thousand million years of history in the rocks

Compared with the 4,000 or so years of human presence, the 2,000,000,000 years of geological history recorded in the rocks of Grand Canyon seems an immeasurable span of time, although it still only represents less than half the age of the Earth.

The oldest rock in the canyon appears in the Inner Gorge: it is a type of metamorphic rock known as "Vishnu Schist" and it is all that remains of an immense mountain chain that existed two thousand million years ago. Above it are heaped numerous rock strata formed of various types of sediment, deposited not only in the depths of the many seas which in the course of time occupied present-day northern Arizona, but also in desert environments characterized by enormous sand dunes.

The first and oldest group of strata – normally in a series of rock layers the oldest are to be found at the bottom and the most recent at the top – is made up mainly of sandstone and clay schist which formed in marine surroundings between one and two thousand million years ago. Gradually a lifting of the crust inclined these strata, originally horizontal, at an angle of 10–12°, as can be seen by examining the walls of the Inner Gorge. This lifting was followed by a period of some 500 million years during which no new sediments were deposited and which ended at

A first glimpse of the Grand Canyon must surely evoke the feeling of the presence of a superior power: there can be no doubt that some awesome force was responsible for the creation of this vast expanse of amazing peaks and chasms. Multiple levels of intricate rock formations, stretching into the far distance, rise up from the immense floor of the canyon as if in accordance with a pre-ordained plan. The jagged upper rim of the canyon reflects the winding course of the Colorado River which, about 70 million years ago, began its slow work of eroding the successive rock strata.

PICNIC AREAS AND CAMPGROUNDS

In the South Rim sector there are five picnic areas with facilities along East Rim Drive, one in Grand Canyon Village and one at Desert View. In the North Rim sector there are two along State Highway 67, one near Grand Canyon Lodge and one for each of the three most important viewpoints: Point Imperial, Vista Encantadora and Cape Royal. In the South Rim sector there are also two campgrounds for tents, one at Desert View ($6 per night, closed in winter, no advance booking) and one in Grand Canyon Village (Mather Campground, $8 per night): both are equipped with toilets, showers and running water; from 15 May to 30 September advance booking is possible for Mather Campground by contacting the Ticketron Reservation Office, PO Box 2715, San Francisco, California 94126. In Grand Canyon Village there is also a Trailer Village, an area specifically for trailers, with toilets, showers, etc. At North Rim there is a campground with 82 places ($6 per night, no advance booking), Numerous other organized campgrounds are situated close to the park. For free camping, application must be made to the Backcountry Reservation Office.

the beginning of the Cambrian (600 million years ago) when a new sea submerged the region. From then until 70 million years ago there was a steady succession of sedimentation and erosion cycles, with the sea rhythmically advancing and receding.

Many strata, especially those of calcareous rock, contain fossil remains of plants and animals that have since vanished and which represent the most interesting pages, as it were, in the history of the Grand Canyon. However, this great story book is full of gaps: erosion has swept away many of the pages and has at the same time prevented others being written, so that in effect the history of the region came to a halt about 70 million years ago when the Colorado River began to cut away the rock strata.

The marked trails

In the Grand Canyon National Park the marked trails are divided into two categories; principal trails, 38 in number, covering some 644 km (402 miles), and 400 secondary trails. The former are in excellent condition, thanks to continual maintenance work, and are constantly patrolled by rangers; the latter, however, are not regularly maintained and demand good powers of orientation. The length of time needed to cover the trails described here takes in the outward and return journeys, where not otherwise specified. All the trails leading down to the bottom of the canyon involve a steep descent and a long, arduous climb.

SOUTH RIM
Principal paths

Rim Trail   E

29 km (18 miles), 10 hours

Begins at Hermit's Rest, at the western tip of West Rim Drive; ends at Yavapai Point. This is an easy, safe and highly spectacular trail which snakes around the edge of the South Rim and passes virtually all the viewpoints of West Rim Drive. Moreover, since it runs almost parallel to the road, it need only be followed for short stretches if preferred, and is actually the most effective introduction to the grandeur of the Grand Canyon. A service vehicle runs along West Rim Drive.

South Kaibab Trail   M

20.5 km (13 miles), 1,500 m (4,950 ft) change in elevation, 12 hours

Begins at Yaki Point, along East Rim Drive not far from Grand Canyon Village; ends at Bright Angel Campground. This trail, completed in 1928, links the two sides of the canyon, by means of a footbridge over the Colorado. It is advisable to do the walk by day, allowing about 4 hours for the outward journey and at least double that for the return. No Backcountry Use Permit is required. About two thirds of the way along it crosses the Tonto Trail.

Bright Angel Trail   M

30.5 km (19 miles), 1,350 m (4,500 ft) change in elevation, 15 hours

Begins at Grand Canyon Village; ends at Bright Angel Campground. This trail, which can also be done on mules, is the most frequent descent route to the Colorado River, snaking down in a long series of broad zigzags. At Indian Gardens (free camping area and rangers' station) it crosses the Tonto Trail. It is advisable to do the journey by day, allowing about 5 hours for the outward trip and at least double that for the return. No Backcountry Use Permit is required.

The eastern end of the South Rim can be seen clearly by taking the road which leads to Page and Marble Canyon. At this point the canyon is extremely narrow, cutting like filigree work into the flat surface of the mesa and forming an interesting graphic effect.

Overleaf: the muddy appearance of the Colorado River and its excavating role within the canyon are clearly visible from the edge of a rock spur or, better still, from a flight in a helicopter which can be booked at Grand Canyon Village.

PLANTS AND ANIMALS OF AN ENTIRE CONTINENT

Each of the altitude belts described under *Climate* (page 15) has its own typical plants and animals, so that a climb from the foot of the canyon to the Kaibab Plateau in the North Rim sector is equivalent to a journey across the entire North American continent from Mexico to Hudson Bay.

Typical desert plants grow in the Lower Sonoran zone, including various species of cactus, agave and yucca, together with shrubs such as mesquite (*Prosopis* spp.), ocotillo (*Fouquieria splendens*, illustrated right) and creosote (*Larrea divaricata*). Broadleaved trees are represented by willows and poplars which line the banks of watercourses. Perfectly camouflaged among the rocks, thanks to its salmon-pink coloration, the Grand Canyon rattlesnake (*Crotalus* sp.), which feeds on small animals, is one of many reptile species living in this arid zone. Mammals have, for the most part, developed nocturnal habits to avoid the sunniest, hottest times of day; this is the case with the mule deer (*Odocoileus hemionus*), which comes down from higher zones to drink, and the much rarer bighorn (*Ovis canadensis*), an ungulate which resembles the European mouflon and is a typical inhabitant of mountain areas with little vegetation. The birds, on the other hand, are mainly diurnal by habit, sheltering in the foliage of the few trees or in the shade of rocks during the hottest parts of the day. Among the spectacular hummingbirds, which sip nectar with their long bills, the most common is *Selasphorus rufus*.

Passing upwards through the Upper Sonoran and Transition zones, the characteristic trees of the former are the nut pine (*Pinus edulis*) and Utah juniper (*Juniperus osteosperma*), and of the latter the western yellow pine (*P. ponderosa*). These environments are very similar to those of other parks in the southwestern United States both in their flora and fauna constituents. The only important exception is Abert's squirrel (*Sciurus aberti*), which is found along the South Rim, and the Kaibab squirrel (*S. kaibabensis*), confined to the North Rim. Both species live together in forests of yellow pine and are almost identical in behaviour and appearance, apart from the tail, which in the former is grey or blackish above and in the latter completely white. These squirrels originally belonged to a single species but as the canyon became deeper they were divided into two isolated groups which in time gave rise to two new species.

The South Rim sector is characterized by Upper Sonoran and Transition climatic and vegetational belts, whereas the North Rim comes into the Canadian category. Here the soil is richer and deeper, supporting two distinct types of forest (one spruce-fir-poplar, the other western yellow pine) and broad prairies, the ideal habitat for many small mammals (shrews, voles, wild mice, mustelids, etc.). Among the bigger mammals are the ubiquitous mule deer, the coyote (*Canis latrans*), the porcupine (*Erethizon dorsatum*) and, very occasionally, the puma (*Felis concolor*); birds include woodpeckers of the genus *Colaptes*, the rare wild turkey (*Meleagris gallopavo*), the blue grouse (*Dendragapus obscurus*) and the great horned owl (*Bubo virginianus*). Finally, on the highest peaks of the North Rim, above 2,800 m (9,000 ft), the climate is again much harsher, the flora and fauna are impoverished and the surroundings take on the features typical of the subarctic belt.

PHOTOGRAPHIC HINTS

Anyone who visits the Grand Canyon will be eager to capture something of its grandeur and wonder on camera. For wide-angle photography you will need a foreground subject in order to convey some idea of proportion, given the huge distance between one rim and the other. For this type of shot the entire wall of the canyon as it appears in the viewfinder must be well illuminated, and consequently the best times are when there is full daylight, avoiding, of course, midday.

Interesting pictures can be taken by zooming in at interesting angles, using lenses of between 100 and 200 mm focal length and making sure to frame well in the viewfinder the succession of rock spurs and terraces. Guaranteed effects can be obtained after sunset when the rocks, as a result of the atmospheric veiling, take on a bluish tinge.

Telephoto lenses can be used for taking excellent pictures of the canyon floor, particularly when shot from a helicopter.

Secondary trails

It is advisable to use secondary trails only after testing one's physical condition on the South Kaibab or Bright Angel Trails.

Grandview Trail   M

9.5 km (6 miles), about 800 m (2,650 ft) change in elevation, 6 hours

Begins at Grandview Point, along East Rim Drive; ends at the Horseshoe Mesa. Short walk which joins the Tonto Trail west of the Horseshoe Mesa.

Tanner Trail D

25.5 km (16 miles), about 1,400 m (4,600 ft), 14 hours

Begins some 100 m (100 yards) east of Lipan Point, along East Rim Drive; ends at Tanner Rapids on the Colorado River. The trail, which runs through Tanner Canyon, was once used by horse thieves to cross from Arizona into Utah, where the animals were sold.

At some points the trail is indistinct but low heaps of stones mark the path. On Grandview Trail and this one there is no water and in summer you should take some along.

Strange and remarkable colour effects can be observed in the erosion zones close to the river. The succession of low hills along the banks have taken on a violet tinge and in places are reminiscent of the typical landscape of the Painted Desert.

Hermit Trail   D

27.4 km (17 miles), about 1,300 m (4,300 ft) change in elevation, 14 hours

Begins at Hermit's Rest, at the western extremity of West Rim Drive; ends at Hermit Rapids on the Colorado River. The trail, though it requires experience and training, presents no particular difficulties. The last part of the trail runs alongside Hermit Creek which it reaches after following a tract of the Tonto Trail to the west.

New Hance Trail   D

25.5 km (16 miles), 1,400 m (4,700 ft) change in elevation, 14 hours

Begins about 1.5 km (1 mile) west of Moran Point, along East Rim Drive; ends at Hance Rapids on the Colorado River. This is a very arduous trail, not to be attempted in a single day. At many points the path almost disappears and considerable orientational ability and experience are needed to follow it, aided at intervals by piles of marking stones. Some stretches are steep and rocky, requiring extreme care.

Boucher Trail   D

35.3 km (22 miles), 1,300 m (4,300 ft) change in elevation, minimum 2 days

Begins at Hermit's Rest, at the western extremity of West Rim Drive; ends at Boucher Creek. This is one of the park's easier trails although it needs orientational ability. This first section coincides with Hermit Trail and you have to branch off, along Dripping Springs Trail, to reach the start of Boucher Trail proper. At some points the trail seems to vanish and it is advisable to proceed, especially downhill, only when you have spotted the next heap of stones. Before terminating in the normally dry bed of Boucher Creek, which can be followed along the bank to the Colorado, the path crosses the Tonto Trail.

Tonto Trail   D

116 km (72 miles), minimum 4 days

Begins at the meeting point with the New Hance Trail (Red Canyon); ends at Garnet Canyon. The

On the previous page: the Painted Desert is situated in the northern part of the Petrified Forest National Park. Its hills bear traces of iron which emerge from the strata of clay and sandstone as "painted" marks that vary in colour from bright red to pale blue.

trail runs from east to west along the inside of the Grand Canyon, continuing without significant changes in elevation across Tonto Plateau, a huge terrace-like strip of desert suspended between the South Rim above and the Colorado River below. Although it is seldom followed for its entire length, it conveniently interlinks a number of trails which run down from the South Rim to the foot of the canyon.

NORTH RIM
Principal trails

North Kaibab Trail   D

35.3 km (22 miles), about 1,700 m (5,580 ft) change in elevation, 3 days

Begins at the North Rim; ends at Bright Angel Campground, near the Colorado River. The trail is long but not difficult, although for the first 7.5 km (4¾ miles) the descent is fairly steep. At the confluence of Bright Angel Creek and Roaring Springs Canyon there are pools which are safe for bathing.

At sunset the light strikes the spurs of rock, creating a fascinating interplay of light and shade.

Clear Creek Trail   D

29 km (18 miles), about 400 m (1,320 ft) change in elevation, 2 days

Begins at Phantom Ranch; ends at Clear Creek. This trail, which branches off the North Kaibab Trail near Phantom Ranch, crosses the Tonto Plateau and two intermittent streams before terminating on the bank of Clear Creek. Here it is possible, having previously obtained a license, to fish for trout; the cold waters of the stream are an ideal habitat for these fish which swim up the Colorado when it becomes muddy. It is also possible to go farther, ascending Clear Creek for about 12 km (7½ miles) to Chevaya Falls, which are particularly impressive in spring.

Other trails

Starting at the North Rim campground, other trails can be followed, including the short Transept Trail; the panoramic Widforss Trail, which skirts the southern edge of the Kaibab Plateau; the Ken Patrick Trail, which leads to Point Imperial; the Uncle Jim Trail and the longer Tiyo Point Trail.

VIEWPOINTS

Given the Grand Canyon's enormous dimensions and marked changes of elevation, the first and most immediate impact has to be visual. This must have been obvious to the planners of the park who, without unnecessarily disfiguring the landscape, ensured that there was easy access to certain spots from which visitors could enjoy a rich diversity of panoramas. Along the South Rim the best points for watching dawn and sunset are Pima, Hopi, Havapai, Yaki and Lipan, while in the North Rim the ideal spot is Bright Angel Point. For views of the Colorado River running through the bottom of the canyon the choice is between Hopi, Mohave, Lipan, Pima and Desert View. Marvellous long-distance views of the Painted Desert can be enjoyed from Vista Encantadora, Walhalla Overlook and Cape Royal, all in the North Rim.

HUMPHREY'S PEAK

Access: from the town of Flagstaff, 127 km (80 miles) south of Grand Canyon Village by US 180.
Points of interest: At 3,862 m (12,667 ft), this is the highest peak of the San Francisco mountain range and in the whole of Arizona. It is in the Kaibab National Forest, an area of considerable local importance.

MONUMENT VALLEY TRIBAL PARK

Access: 290 km (181 miles) east of Grand Canyon Village, by State Highway 24, US 89, US 160 and US 163, on the border of Arizona and Utah.
Points of interest: This tribal park of 1,192 km² (460 sq. miles) forms part of the huge Navajo Indian reserve, which was opened in 1958 to conserve that tribe's history and culture, and contains some of the most spectacular and beautiful scenery in the world. Monument Valley (illustrated below and on the following spread), with its strange, monument-like rocky outcrops (mesas and buttes) has often been the setting for Western films and strip cartoons. The park has a Visitor Center, open May–September from 7.00 am to 7.00 pm and October–April from 8.00 am to 5.00 pm, and an organized campground (100 places, no advance booking, open October–April). 10 km (6¼ miles) west of the Visitor Center is the Goulding Trading Post complex which offers accommodation, shopping and other services throughout the year. A dirt road runs 27 km (17 miles) through the park, affording the opportunity of a quick visit. Local guides organize trips

of various kinds. For information apply to the Superintendent, Box 93, Monument Valley, Utah 84536, tel. (801) 727-3287.

Photographic hints: The most dramatic and colourful effects are to be had at sunset, when the tufts of grass and green shrubs in the foreground form a vivid contrast with the golden-orange of the rocks. The characteristic mesas, seen in countless westerns, rearing up like towers and skyscrapers, can be taken very effectively with a 300 mm telephoto lens.

CANYON DE CHELLY NATIONAL MONUMENT

Access: About 400 km (250 miles) east of Grand Canyon Village, by State Highway 64, US 89, US 160, State Highway 264 and US 191. Only some 200 km (125 miles) southeast of Monument Valley Tribal Park.

Points of interest: The high, jutting walls of red sandstone of the Canyon de Chelly and the Canyon del Muerto, which together make up a protected area of 336 km^2 (130 sq. miles), conceal ruins of Indian settlements which date back to A.D. 350. The area contains a Visitor Center, a campground (free, open all year round, no water November–March), a hotel-restaurant (Thunderbird Lodge, Box 548, Chinle, Arizona 86503, tel. (602) 674-5443, low season 15 November–28 February). Other services can be found in the nearby town of Chinle. Two paved roads of about 18 km (11 miles) skirt the two canyons and provide easy access to a number of viewpoints. The

White House Ruins Trail (2½ hours outward and return) is the only easily negotiable trail (a guide is available at the Visitor Center); other trails can be covered on foot or by minor tracks only if accompanied by a local Navajo guide. The rangers organize nature and archaeological hikes and give evening talks throughout the year. Horse rides and motor trips can also be arranged. For detailed information apply to the Visitor Center, tel. (602) 674-5436, open from 8 am to 5 pm, or to the Superintendent, Canyon de Chelly National Monument, PO Box 588, Chinle, Arizona 86503.

PETRIFIED FOREST NATIONAL PARK

Access: The south entrance is 170 km (106 miles) east of Flagstaff, about 300 km (187 miles) from Grand Canyon Village; the north entrance is about 140 km (87 miles) south of the Canyon de Chelly National Monument. Entrance charge of $5 per car; Golden Eagle Passport valid.

Points of interest: This arid tableland, once a vast plain cut through by rivers and covered with forests of giant trees, is today a unique open-air museum. Some of the ancient tree trunks, together with dinosaur remains, were fossilized about 200 million years ago as a result of a lengthy process which transformed them into hard and brightly coloured silica (the so-called Petrified Forest). The park was opened with the specific aim of preserving these trunks *in situ* and of protecting the surrounding territory, one of the loveliest areas of which is the Painted Desert. The Visitor Center is situated at the north entrance, while the Rainbow Forest Museum serves as the information center for the south entrance. Near the former are a restaurant and service station; other services and facilities for overnight stays are

available in nearby towns. There are no campgrounds in the park but free camping is allowed (the necessary permit is free of charge and available from both information centers). A paved road of 43 km (27 miles) crosses the park from the north to south entrances, taking in the most interesting places which are served by short trails; the first stretch of road contains some eight viewpoints for admiring the Painted Desert. Off-trail trips can be made through the Painted Desert and on Puerco Ridge; in addition to a permit, you will need maps and a plentiful supply of water, which is available only in areas of the park with proper facilities. For detailed information write to or telephone the Superintendent, Petrified Forest National Park, PO Box 217, Arizona 86028, tel. (602) 524-6228.

Photographic hints: The Petrified Forest and the Painted Desert offer opportunities for dramatic and interesting photographs, highlights being the former's siliceous trunks (illustrated below and opposite) and the colourfully banded hills which have given the desert its name.

CALIFORNIA

DEATH VALLEY
NATIONAL MONUMENT

Lying on the borders of California and Nevada, immediately north of the Mojave Desert, Death Valley is one of the hottest and driest places in the world. This huge desert basin, despite its sinister name, offers visitors some astonishing multicoloured rock landscapes and surroundings that teem with life: more than 900 plant species, a myriad of insects and other invertebrates, one of the largest populations in the United States of bighorn sheep, numerous other mammals, 230 species of birds, many of them migratory, reptiles and fish. The story of the people who have lived there or tried to live there is equally fascinating.

From prehistory to white settlement

At first glimpse, it appears inconceivable that man ever managed to live in Death Valley prior to the development of modern technology which helps, at least in part, to make torrid heat and extreme drought endurable. Yet a quite different picture emerges from archaeological research: some unmistakable traces have been found of at least four prehistoric cultures, the oldest of which goes back to about 5000 B.C. Much more recent was the arrival in the valley of the Shoshone Indians, around A.D. 1000, and it was in 1849 that they saw the first white men who ventured, by mistake, into their territory.

The Shoshone had developed a very simple way of life but it enabled them to survive in these very hostile surroundings. As hunters and gatherers they ate the seeds of the mesquite and of the cones produced by the pines which grew on the hills around

Address: Superintendent, Death Valley National Monument, Death Valley, California 92238, tel. (619) 786-2331.
Area: 8,090 km² (3,124 sq. miles).
Altitude: From 86 m (282 ft) below sea level to 3,368 m (11,047 ft) above sea level.
Access: By various state roads which connect to the west with Interstate 395, to the east with Interstate 95 and to the south with Interstate 15.
Opening times: All year round, 24 hours a day.
Entry charge: $5 per car, $2 per pedestrian or bicycle; Golden Eagle Passport valid.

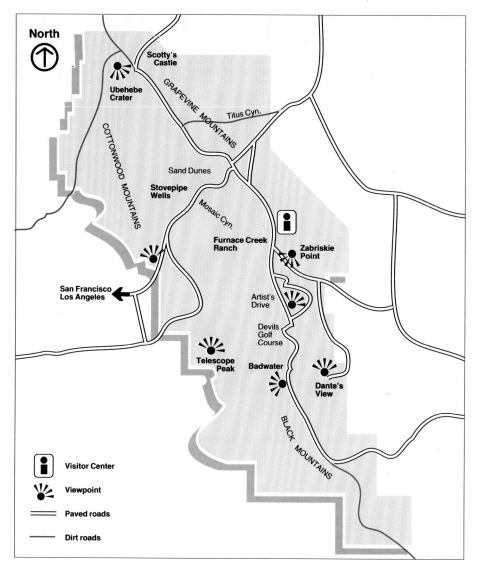

North

Scotty's Castle

Ubehebe Crater

GRAPEVINE MOUNTAINS

Titus Cyn.

COTTONWOOD MOUNTAINS

Sand Dunes

Stovepipe Wells

Mosaic Cyn.

Furnace Creek Ranch

Zabriskie Point

San Francisco Los Angeles

Artist's Drive

Devils Golf Course

Telescope Peak

Badwater

Dante's View

BLACK MOUNTAINS

Visitor Center

Viewpoint

Paved roads

Dirt roads

Fuel and Shops: At Furnace Creek, Scotty's Castle and Stovepipe Wells Village.
Roads: The park is crossed by paved and dirt roads, some suitable only for four-wheel drives or pedestrians.
Accommodation: Various alternatives at Furnace Creek and Stovepipe Wells (some establishments open only in winter); for information and advance booking contact Fred Harvey Inc., PO Box 187, Death Valley, Califor-nia 92238, tel. (619) 786-2345, and the Reservations Depart-ment, Death Valley, California 92238, tel. (619) 786-2387.
Visitor Center: Situated at Fur-nace Creek, it offers permanent exhibitions, audio-visual mate-rial, books, maps and informa-tion; from 1 November to Easter it is open from 8 am to 8 pm, and during the remainder of the year from 8 am to 5 pm.
Viewpoints: Dante's View, Aguereberry Point and Zabriskie Point can all be reached by car.
Guided tours: In winter the park naturalists organize daily excur-sions and evening talks; for de-tailed programme apply to the Visitor Center.
Other activities: Tour operators organize sightseeing trips, some of them off-trail (enquire at Visi-tor Center); it is also possible to arrange outings on horseback and by bicycle, and games of golf.
Beware of: High temperatures and lack of water.

the valley, supplementing their diet with the flesh of mice, rabbits and bighorns. Too busy to fight for survival, the Shoshone were never a warlike tribe and faced with the arrival of the first pioneers they reacted as they had always done when invaded: they went into hiding.

The first pioneers

The saga of the forty-niners is one of the most eventful episodes in the history of the conquest of the Wild West by the white man. During the period of the Gold Rush two family groups, the Bennetts and the Arcans, headed for California in search of a fortune, and decided to let their guide follow a short-cut marked on their map. This decision soon proved disastrous; the short-cut did not actually exist and they found themselves, in midwinter, dangerously short of provisions in the very heart of Death Valley. They entrusted their last hopes to two young men, William Lewis Manly and John Haney Rogers who, taking along with them all the money and the few provisions that remained, set off in search of food. The pair, who almost died in the attempt, trekked more than 400 km (250 miles) across deserts, mountains and canyons before finding a ranch, eventually returning in wagons with the necessary supplies. On arrival they found their forty-seven companions, including women and children, at the end of their tether but still alive. The fact that it was winter was probably the only reason they survived. The story ends by telling how one of the forty-niners, having reached the summit of the Panamint Range, turned towards the valley and said, "Goodbye, Death Valley," superseding for ever the old Shoshone name for the area "Tomesha," meaning "ground afire."

The mining era

Shortly after the forty-niners quit Death Valley, numerous gold-rushers explored the region in the hope of finding precious metals there. Sporadic rumours of the discovery of gold continued to attract adventurers but all searches were in vain. Mute testimony to the stubborn endeavours of countless men is to be seen in the pits and ruins of certain "ghost towns."

USEFUL ADVICE

Because of the enormous size of the area and the harsh environmental conditions, it is essential to plan your activities precisely, whether touring by car or on foot.

For automobile excursions, given the vast distances and the absence of public facilities, you absolutely must make sure that the car is in perfect running order, that there is plenty of fuel and that the water in the radiator is topped up to the maximum. To cope with the frequent occurrence of engines overheating, tanks of *non-drinkable* water are positioned along the paved roads of the park. The sitings of these are marked with a red dot on the map which is given away free at the entrance. In the event of a breakdown do not for any reason abandon the car or wander away from the road, but notify other passing drivers of the problem and wait on the spot for help.

In summer many dirt roads are closed to motor traffic: in fact, because the valley is seldom visited by motorists in the hottest months, there is a real danger, should you have an accident or breakdown, of having to wait several days before anyone else happens to pass by.

Again, during the summer, problems related to heat and drought are naturally aggravated, so before setting out be sure to read the pamphlet *Hot Weather Hints*, available at the entrances, the Visitor Center and all the Ranger Stations, and follow its instructions to the letter.

From the climatic viewpoint, the most favourable period is between October and April, even though the park tends to be very crowded, especially around Christmas, New Year and Easter. If you want to avoid hordes of people you will have to choose other dates or opt for the summer, when there are few visitors and the inconvenience of searing heat is offset by the delights of silence and solitude.

PICNIC AREAS AND CAMPGROUNDS

There are three fully-equipped picnic areas: one is situated at the Sand Dunes, another along the paved road that connects Wildrose Campground to the Panamint Valley Road, and the third at Scotty's Castle.

Of the nine official campgrounds, three are open all year round: Furnace Creek (maximum stay 14 days), Mesquite Spring and Wildrose; another three are open from November to April (Texas Spring, Sunset and Stovepipe Wells), while the rest (Emigrant, Thorndike and Mahogany) are open March–April to October–November. None of the campgrounds can be booked in advance. For further information write to the Superintendent, asking for the pamphlet *Camping in Death Valley*.

No permission is needed for free camping, but it is nevertheless advisable to notify the rangers; regulations applicable to free camping sites are listed in the pamphlet *Dirt road travel and backcountry camping in Death Valley National Monument*, also obtainable by mail.

The only mining activity not to meet with failure was the extraction of borax, nicknamed "white gold of the desert," which began around 1880 and, with various ups and downs, continues to this day. The discovery of this mineral, used in many different industrial processes (glass, porcelain, fertilizers, etc.) has passed into legend, and especially noted are the almost superhuman efforts that were needed at that time to transport the material from Furnace Creek to Mojave, 265 km (165 miles) farther south. The journey along a track especially built for the purpose was made by a team of twenty mules, and it took them ten to twelve days to haul the load of 36.5 tons.

In 1933, during the longest recorded interruption of borax extraction, Death Valley was designated a protected area as a National Monument. Even then the valley was famous all over the States, not only because of the odyssey of the forty niners but also for the bizarre "Scotty's Castle," a luxurious and expensive Spanish-style ranch built by a Chicago financier, Albert Johnson, and his legendary friend Walter Scott, better known as Death Valley Scotty. Today the castle belongs to the National Park Service and is open to the public, but it retains its fascination as a somewhat kitsch symbol of the fruitless attempts to tame Death Valley.

SHORT TRIPS

The moon-like surface of Death Valley, only apparently devoid of life, is crossed by a few marked trails, old tracks and dirt roads which provide the chance to visit on foot places of particular natural and historic interest. Although the walks are very short, lasting only one or two hours, it is advisable always to carry a good stock of water and to wear strong shoes. The length of time mentioned for the trails described below comprises the outward and return journeys.

Self-guiding trails

Almost all the marked paths are "self-guiding" or "interpretive" trails, so called because in every instance there is a small guide, obtainable from the Visitor Center, which provides detailed explanations of everything to be found along the way.

Harmony Borax Works Trail   E

0.4 km (¼ mile)

About 3 km (1¾ miles) north of the Visitor Center, near the paved road, this extremely short trail encircles the ruins of the first settlements for the extraction of borax.

Zabriskie Point has emerged as virtually the symbol of Death Valley; in this context its dunes served as the natural setting for the film of that name by the Italian director Michelangelo Antonioni. The visual fascination of this lunar landscape arouses strong emotions: whereas other parks to the west attract visitors for their beauty, every corner of Death Valley evokes the spirit of the old Wild West. Visitors to the valley cannot fail to think of the pioneers who travelled across the area over a century ago on their way to find fortune in California.

Overleaf: a view from the air of the Funeral Mountains at sunset; the rock structure is clearly visible in the sunlight.

CLIMATE

The park has a desert climate, with very high temperatures and low precipitation. The hottest month is August, with a maximum average temperature on the valley floor of 43.5°C (110°F); at night the heat subsides and the temperature drops to 29°C (84°F). During the other summer months, June, July and September, the temperature climbs during the hottest part of the day to over 38°C (100°F).

The best season for making any sort of trip in the park is therefore winter, even though cold winds may prove a nuisance: the coldest month is January when the maximum temperature is around 18°C (64°F) and the minimum about 4°C (39°F). During the entire year there is a marked difference between the temperatures at the bottom of the valley and those of the surrounding mountains: on the top of Telescope Peak the thermometer may read as much as 10°C (18°F) less than that of Furnace Creek, at 58 m (190 ft) below sea level.

As regards rainfall, the annual average is only around 38 mm (1½ in), with a maximum in winter and a minimum in summer. Occasionally, however, there may be sudden storms, severe enough to cause floods, and sometimes violent "washes" that sweep down from the heights to the valley floor. Strong and constant winds throughout the year often whip up sandstorms which may force campers to abandon their tents.

The marked aridity of Death Valley is caused not only by the particular morphological features of the area and the atmospheric circulation, but also by the presence, to the west of the park, of the Sierra Nevada, which checks the passage of disturbances from the Pacific and extracts their rain. Death Valley is therefore a so-called "rain-shadow desert." Indeed the highest temperature ever registered in Death Valley was 57°C (134°F) and this almost constitutes a world record.

BADWATER AND ARTIST'S DRIVE

Situated close to the lowest point not only of Death Valley but also of the entire western hemisphere – 86 m (282 ft) below sea level – is Badwater, which takes its name from a well of "bad" though not poisonous water fed by a permanent spring. In spite of the water salinity, the well contains both plant and animal organisms; among the latter, and clearly visible, are the larvae of certain flies and bronze-coloured aquatic beetles, which feed on algae. Badwater, ˙ very probably the hottest place on earth, lies south of Furnace Creek along the park's main road and is therefore easily accessible by car. It is also one of the stops on the fascinating "Badwater self-guiding auto tour," which takes in some of the most beautiful and interesting places in the valley. A small guide, sold at the Visitor Center, describes this tour in detail, providing information about the history and wildlife associated with each of the stops on the route (the numbers in the guide correspond to those on the signboards at the roadside). The tour includes Artist's Drive, along which there are four stops where you can see how the geological evolution of the landscape is still in progress. The most spectacular of these is undoubtedly Artist's Palette, with its slabs of multicoloured rock. The origin of this astonishing display of colours is unknown: the reds, yellows, violets, browns and blacks are probably due to the presence of iron oxides, and the greens to the presence of copper and mica, but why this phenomenon should only occur at this one place remains a mystery.

Salt Creek Nature Trail   E

1.6 km (1 mile), 30 minutes

One of the most interesting examples of a nature trail, fully described in the appropriate guide.

A short dirt road, 37 km (23 miles) north of the Visitor Center, leads to the start of this fascinating trail along Salt Creek. There are many fish in the water and numerous birds along the banks. The trail is entirely over wooden walkways so as not to harm the environment.

Golden Canyon Trail   E

3.2 km (2 miles), 1 hour

Begins and ends on the paved road to Badwater, 8 km (5 miles) south of the Visitor Center. The trail climbs gently through the coloured Badlands, a maze of hills and valleys carved by the water in the soft clay deposited at the bottom of an ancient lake that has since disappeared.

The Artist's Palette derives its name from the variety of tonal effects that characterize the rocks which form it. The early and late hours of the day tend to accentuate the intensity of the colours.

Windy Point Trail   E

5.3 km (3¼ miles), 50 m (165 ft) change in elevation, 90 minutes

Begins and ends at Scotty's Castle. A highly panoramic nature trail.

PHOTOGRAPHIC HINTS

For the photographer, as for the attentive observer, Death Valley is much more than an expanse of sand and stone, offering an inexhaustible source of ideas and opportunities for marvellous pictures.

Zabriskie Point is without doubt the most spectacular corner of the valley: it provides ample scope for both wide-angle and telephoto work, notably in the morning towards Telescope Peak and in the afternoon towards Dante's View; the succession of hills with coloured strata provide some highly unusual effects. Sand Dunes afford the chance of experiment in both composition and colour: shots which contrive to combine the illuminated orange tones of the dunes with the grey-blue areas in the shade, if composed correctly, will be predictably dramatic. At Devils Golf Course, pictures taken near ground level with a wide-angle lens can highlight the slabs of salt (see photograph opposite) and at the same time include in the background the peaks of the Panamint Range.

Ubehebe Crater should be photographed when the sun is fairly high so as to avoid the risk of the vertical walls throwing the inside of the crater into complete shadow. A 200 mm telephoto lens, with the lens stopped down to increase the depth of field, can be used to take clumps of mesquite (see photograph below) which form a vivid contrast to the grey-brown background. As the name of the spot suggests, an extraordinary range of colour effects is to be obtained at Artist's Palette. For best results it is advisable to climb to the top of one of the ridges that cuts right across the valley.

For an overall view of Death Valley you must ascend to the summit of Telescope Peak, taking pictures northwards in the morning and eastwards in the afternoon, and using wide-angle lenses suitably polarized to compensate for the haze. Another famous panoramic spot from which good, though less comprehensive, shots can be taken is Dante's View; use a 200 mm telephoto lens for pictures of the salt basin below, where the crust of salt and pools of water combine to create unusual chromatic effects.

FAUNA

The biggest animal to be found in the park is the ass. Strange as it may seem, there is a very large population of wild asses in Death Valley. They are the descendants of pack animals which arrived in the area with the first pioneers and returned to their wild state after being abandoned or running away, proving that they possessed a far greater ability than their masters to adapt to harsh environmental conditions. However, the presence of this attractive animal has not been entirely beneficial; many studies have been conducted to ascertain the nature and amount of the harm done by the species to its surroundings. Originally it was thought to be competing with the bighorn (*Ovis canadensis*), which had always inhabited the zone, but today there is not complete agreement over the findings.

Some researchers maintain that the two animals frequent habitats that are geologically quite distinct and that consequently there are no problems of competition: the ass, indeed, seems deliberately to avoid the areas of carbonated rock (e.g. limestone) because of the severe damage it can do to its hooves, whereas this is the ideal habitat for the bighorns. Others, however, argue that the asses, together with the increasing amount of human activity in the valley, are responsible for the marked decline in numbers of the sheep, as well as for turning new areas into

desert because of their harmful habit of browsing plants.

The bighorn, perfectly adapted to the desert climate, nowadays lives mainly in the mountains and is not an easy animal to approach. The best chances of photographing it, or just of seeing it in its natural surroundings, occur in the Panamint Range and, most of all, on the way up to Telescope Peak.

Among the most common carnivores are the coyote (*Canis latrans*), pictured below, which is perhaps the only animal that regularly crosses the salt basin, and the kit fox (*Vulpes macrotis*), easily recognized by its big ears, which often approaches tents in the evening in search of food and to hunt small rodents. Among the latter, kangaroo rats (*Dipodomys* spp.), white-footed mice (*Peromyscus eremicus*) and various species of ground squirrel (genera *Ammosperophilus* and *Citellus*) are most abundant in the sandy zones where the large mesquite bushes (*Prosopis glandulosa*) offer them shelter.

The dunes colonized by mesquite constitute the ideal habitat, too, for numerous reptiles such as tortoises (*Testudo* spp.), lizards (of which seventeen different species have been counted), and snakes, the most feared of which is the horned rattlesnake (*Crotalus cerastes*), also known as the sidewinder because of the way in which it moves sideways, leaving a series of unmistakable parallel J-shaped prints in the sand. The snake spends the hottest part of the day in the shelter of a shrub or buried in the sand, preferring to hunt small rodents and lizards by night.

The fish population merits special attention for it comprises four endemic species, unique to this area and perfectly adapted to the high salinity level of the water. They are descendants of those fish which remained isolated in spring pools when the watercourses linking Death Valley with the Colorado River were cut off after the deepening of the valley itself, presumably about one million years ago.

The fish measure from 2.5 cm (1 in) to 7.5 cm (3 in) long and live mainly in the springs along the Amargosa River, in the southern sector of the park, with the exception of one species which is found below sea level in pools on the western edge of the Cottonball Basin and in Salt Creek.

Other short trips

There are some canyons which are ideal for easy, untiring walks, with the freedom to go as far as you want and turn back at any time.

LONGER TRAILS

In theory Death Valley offers countless opportunities for long hikes and treks but, because of the scarcity of marked trails and the harsh surroundings, even the experienced and trained walker is in practice restricted. As a rule, the dirt roads suited to four-wheel drives are also ideal for walking and offer a vast range of safe routes, firstly because they present no problems of orientation and secondly because a back-up vehicle can always follow if you prefer. Some trails of this type, together with ascents of the surrounding mountains, are described here. Distances and times comprise outward and return journeys, if not otherwise specified.

Desolation Canyon   E

6.5 km (4 miles)

Begins and ends on the paved road to Badwater, 8 km (5 miles) south of the Visitor Center. The route follows an old road with canyons on either side.

*The turkey vulture (*Cathartes aura*) is distinguished from other members of the family by the colour of its wings: the flight feathers are silver-grey bordered in black. The bird makes long, gliding flights, landing on rock spurs, seldom beating its wings. Adult individuals have a red head while the young are darker. The vulture, feeding principally on carrion and refuse, lives in desert zones.*

On pages 46 and 47: inside Death Valley there are a number of different types of habitat: one of these is made up of the sand dunes, characterized by the fact that their structure continuously changes because of wind action.

A DESERT BELOW SEA LEVEL

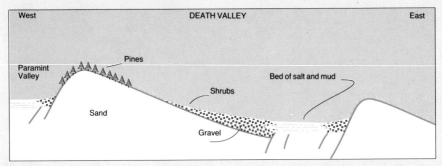

Death Valley is an enormous desert basin characterized by three different types of environment, yet closely interlinked: the mountain chains, the alluvial cones (see photograph opposite) and the playa.

The mountain chains, high and rocky, extend from north to south and constitute the natural boundaries of the valley, beyond which stretch other desert basins. They are young mountains which originated in the course of the last four to five million years of crustal movements, a process which is still continuing. According to the classic model, the crust splits into stiff blocks which subsequently, under the thrust of various forces, are lifted or lowered, respectively forming mountain chains or valleys. Valleys of this type, like Death Valley itself, are described as structural, and differ noticeably from fluvial and/or glacial valleys, typical of mountain chains that are no longer young and which originate from erosion. The Panamint Range to the west and the Black Mountains to the east nevertheless display another characteristic: the walls that face west are high and jagged, whereas those that face east slope gradually downwards to the plain (see drawing above). This is indicative of a rotary movement affecting the crustal blocks from the time of lifting. These complex movements have also caused numerous fractures (faults) in the crust, some of which are hidden beneath the sediments that have accumulated on the valley bottom, while others are clearly visible because they have brought into contact rocks of very different ages. Along the faults, when as in this case they are still active, there is marked seismic activity; geologists reckon that the last devastating earthquake to hit Death Valley occurred not later than 2,000 years ago.

The alluvial cones move down from the sides of mountains and spread out, rather like giant fans, on the valley floor. There are various forms of these but all have the same origin: during the Quaternary glaciations much more water than today, which came from distant ice-covered regions, coursed through the area. The rivers were then certainly powerful enough to erode large quantities of rock which were carried down in the turbulent descent to the valley, so that initially the bigger stones were deposited there and then gradually the smaller ones. In fact the so-called alluvial cones are made up of more or less coarse material (gravel, sand and lime) transported and deposited by the water: the shape of the stones, rounded or sharply pointed, depends above all on the type of rock of which they are made, while the alluvial-fan deposition is the result of changes in direction effected by the watercourses during floods.

At the foot of the cones, the vast desert plain of Death Valley extends for more than 500 km² (193 sq. miles): in geology this terrain is known as the playa, and it is actually the dried bed of an ancient lake, consisting mainly of mud and covered with a hard crust of salt. In fact several such lakes have occupied the surfaces of Death Valley in the course of the last couple of million years. Examination of the remains of ancient lines of beach and river deltas has made it possible to reconstruct the shape and depth (182 m/600 ft) of this Pleistocene Lake, dating from the earlier part of the Quaternary era when the major glaciations occurred. At the end of this period, some 10,000 years ago, the earth's climate changed again; the ice melted and the valley was transformed into the present arid playa, partially refilled with water only as a result of several climatic fluctuations or rare inundations. Today the salt basin collects the little rain which is not immediately absorbed by the soil and water which flows out at the foot

of the mountains. Many springs, however, yield water that is particularly rich in mineral salts which, as a result of high evaporation and complete lack of water exchange (the valley is an internal basin with no outlets), are concentrated on the spot to an extent that they crystallize and form crusts measuring from a few centimeters to several meters in thickness. There are samples of some forty mineral salts in Death Valley: the first to precipitate are the carbonates, which are the least soluble, followed by the sulphates and finally, when maximum concentration is reached, the chlorides, the most common of which is sodium chloride (NaCl), the familiar kitchen salt.

SAND DUNES AND DEVIL'S CORNFIELD

Not far from Stovepipe Wells Village, where the two main roads of the park cross, are two particularly interesting landscape features, situated quite close together: Sand Dunes and the Devil's Cornfield.

The Sand Dunes, typifying the popular concept of a desert, cover a single area of only 39 km² (15 sq. miles), under 5 per cent of the land surface of the entire valley. It lies between the Cottonwood Mountains to the west, Salt Creek to the east and Tucki Mountain to the south, where the concurrence of various factors (arrangement and form of mountains, and seasonal variations in wind direction) cause the sand to accumulate from year to year.

Contrary to appearances, this zone is not devoid of life, as testified by the tracks left in the sand by many animals which find food and shelter in the shrubby plants which have colonized the area. Moreover, the dunes, provided you take sufficient care, offer excellent opportunities for rambling. The appearance of the landscape changes according to the time of day and the intensity and angle of the sun's rays, unexpectedly assuming different forms and colours. A detailed information sheet on the Sand Dunes is obtainable from the Visitor Center.

South of the Sand Dunes, as you approach the salt basin, there is an almost regular succession of diverse vegetational zones, indicating the gradual change in environmental conditions. A typical example is the Devil's Cornfield, adjoining State Highway 190, which derives its name from the characteristic sheaf-like appearance of clumps of *Pluchea sericea*. This phreatophyte grows freely in the salt basin where the salinity of the soil and the water is around 1 per cent, and forms virtually pure associations with an optimum density of seventy-five to one hundred plants per acre.

Salt Creek-McLean Spring　　　E

8 km (5 miles)

The first tract coincides with the Salt Creek Nature Trail, already described. Where the walkways end, the path continues over rough ground for some 3 km (1¾ miles) to McLean Spring, the source of Salt Creek.

Golden Canyon-Zabriskie Point　　M

8 km (5 miles)

Begins at Golden Canyon; ends at the parking lot of the Golden Canyon Trail. A path branching off from the marked trail runs through Golden Canyon, ascending its wall to reach Zabriskie Point, one of the most fascinating places in the entire park. From here the return path crosses Gower Gulch (a dry stream) and eventually meets the road to Badwater just south of the parking lot. The walk can also be done in the opposite direction.

Grotto Canyon　　M

13 km (8 miles)

A dirt road leaves State Highway 190 4 km (2½ miles) east of Stovepipe Wells and after 2.4 km (1½ miles) reaches the entrance of Grotto Canyon. The route continues inside the canyon where for 800 m (almost ½ mile) there are dry falls.

Wildrose Peak Trail　　M

13 km (8 miles)

Begins near Charcoal Kilns, about 11 km (6¾ miles) from the Wildrose Campground; ends at the summit of Wildrose Peak (2,760 m/9,053 ft). This climb to one of the highest peaks in the Panamint Range is not arduous, and has a splendid view of the valley beneath, especially in the afternoon. The trail runs through pine and juniper woodland.

Titus Canyon Narrows　　M

17.7 km (11 miles)

The entrance to the canyon can be reached by a dirt road 3.2 km (2 miles) in length, which branches off Scotty's Castle Road about 60 km (37½ miles) north of the Visitor Center. The road winds for some 7 km (4½ miles) between the high walls of the canyon as far as Klare Spring, where there are traces of petroglyphs on the rock.

On pages 54 and 55: one of the most astounding sights of Death Valley is a vast stretch of salt which, at first glance, could be mistaken for a field of snow.

Telescope Peak Trail   M/D

22.5 km (14 miles), 868 m (2,850 ft) change in elevation

Begins at Mahogany Flat Compound (2,500 m/8,250 ft); ends at summit of Telescope Peak (3,368 m/11,047 ft). This is one of the finest climbs in the park. Pines and junipers grow alongside the trail and the panoramic view from the peak takes in the whole of Death Valley and also the adjoining Panamint Valley. In winter crampons and pickaxes are necessary.

Cottonwood and Marble Canyons   D

40 km (25 miles), minimum 2 days

This trail follows neither roads nor paths, so it is absolutely essential to use a map, obtainable from the Visitor Center. The trek begins where the road for jeeps ends in Cottonwood Canyon and then takes a circular route.

UBEHEBE CRATER

In the most northerly sector of the park, about 15 km (9½ miles) from Scotty's Castle, is a group of volcanoes, of which Ubehebe Crater (pictured below) is the largest and also the youngest. It is thought to be several hundred years old but the last signs of activity, correlated with seismic events, go back less than 200 years. The eruption which created Ubehebe (the name means "clump" in the language of the Shoshone Indians) was so violent that it shot ash and stony fragments into the air at a speed of more than 160 km (100 miles) per hour. Falling to the ground, this material formed a huge greyish-brown blanket around the crater in which water, within a few centuries, has cut deep grooves.

FLORA

Because of the extremely dry surroundings in Death Valley, plant distribution is more than elsewhere strictly dependent upon climatic and geological factors. The former determine the temperatures and the amount of atmospheric precipitation, while the latter dictate the chemical composition of the substratum and the presence or absence of water in the soil. The result is that in Death Valley, too, there are distinct and significant vegetational zones. The summit of Telescope Peak (3,368 m/11,047 ft) and the highest mountains of the Panamint Range fall within the Canadian Zone, characterized by the presence of bristlecone pine (*Pinus aristata*) and limber pine (*P. flexilis*); this vegetational belt is the highest to be encountered in the park, for there are no Alpine and Hudsonian Zones. At lower levels, in the absence of a Transition Zone, the Upper Sonoran Zone is divided into two sub-zones; the first comprises woods of single-leaf piñon (*Pinus monophylla*) and juniper (*Juniperus* spp.), and the second, larger and at a lower level, is notable for various shrub species. Below about 1,200 m (4,000 ft) the Sonoran Zone extends as a cover to

the lower mountain slopes and the alluvial cones down to the valley floor. It is almost wholly devoid of trees, due to the absence of fresh water, and the most representative species is the creosote bush (*Larrea tridentata*).

Whereas up to a certain height it is the climatic factors that play the preponderant role in the distribution of plants, in the cone areas and at the bottom of the valley the chemical and physical characteristics of the substratum carry more weight. The different species thus tend to grow systematically according to the availability and salinity of the water, producing a characteristic form of distribution at the edge of the salt basin which, in turn, is practically devoid of vegetation (under one bush per acre).

Two categories of woody plants may be distinguished on the basis of recognizable differences in the supply of water: the phreatophytes, which flourish where the water table remains close enough to the surface throughout the year to be accessible to their long root system, and the xerophytes, plants which grow in terrain with very little water thanks to certain adaptations which

enable them to survive long periods of drought. It follows, for example, that xerophytes grow among the cones which have been formed by pebbles and coarse materials, where the water table is low, whereas phreatophytes prosper at the foot of the cones and on the rim of the salt basin, where the water table lies only a few centimeters below the surface of the ground.

Among the xerophytes, the sturdiest is the desert holly (*Atriplex hymenelytra*), which grows in the warmer, drier and saltier portions of the cones, forming broad stretches of shrubs, particularly north and east of the salt basin; almost as tough is the creosote bush, a typical plant of the Lower Sonoran Zone and abundantly distributed in Death Valley.

The phreatophytes are more sensitive to salts in water and consequently it has been possible to categorize the species according to their tolerance of salinity. Some, including the willows (*Salix* spp.) and the ditch reed (*Phragmites communis*), grow only in the vicinity of freshwater springs, while nine different species flourish around the salt basin. Of these, the least tolerant is the honey mesquite (*Prosopis juniflora*), which grows where the salt content is very low (only a few hundred parts per million), while at the other extreme of the scale is the pickleweed (*Allenrolfea occidentalis*), which grows freely where salinity reaches 6 per cent, very much higher than that of the ocean.

All these plants have in the course of their evolution developed special morphological and physiological features which ensure that they are not "poisoned" by the salts dissolved in the water. This notwithstanding, slight modifications, such as those caused by human presence during the nineteenth century, have lowered or varied the salinity, causing the death of many plants and seriously compromising the natural equilibrium, with long-term consequences that are difficult to predict.

In addition to these woody species, low and shrubby in habit, there are in Death Valley green algae, found in pools of water, and many annual plants which after spring rainfall germinate and grow with extraordinary speed, so that vast areas are covered in flowers, transforming the desert momentarily into a luxuriant garden.

MONO BASIN

NATIONAL FOREST SCENIC AREA

To the east of Yosemite National Park, in the Mono Basin district, tucked between the Sierra Nevada and chains of young volcanoes, lies Mono Lake, the only one of its kind in the world. "A country of wonderful contrasts. Hot deserts bounded by snow-laden mountains – cinders and ashes scattered on glacier-polished pavements – frost and fire working together in the making of beauty." This was how, more than a century ago, the naturalist John Muir described the landscape of Mono Lake, which he visited on his first trip to Yosemite. Since then many things have changed. The waters feeding the lake have been diverted to assuage the thirst of Los Angeles, threatening to transform it into a salty, lifeless pond, but despite all this it has not lost its fascination.

The same old story

The lands around Mono Lake were once the country of an Indian Paiute tribe known as the Kuzedika. This name was given to them by neighbouring tribes because they were "eaters of the larvae of flies," notably the larvae and pupae of the brine fly which, dried in the sun, constituted a very nutritious and tasty food called *kutsavi*. The diet was supplemented by pinecones and the meat of the bighorn and the pronghorn, in addition to other plants which they obtained in exchange with the Indians who lived in the Sierra Nevada. In fact, *kutsavi*, together with obsidian, salt and pinecones, were much in demand for trading.

Around the middle of the nineteenth century white men invaded the banks of Mono Lake ever

Address: Inyo National Forest, Mono Lake Ranger District, Lee Vining, California 93541, tel. (619) 647-6525.
Area: About 550 km² (212 sq. miles).
Altitude: 1,950 m (6,396 ft) above sea level.
Access: from north and south on Interstate 395; from the nearby Yosemite National Park, on State 120.
Opening times: Throughout the year, 24 hours a day.
Entry charge: Free.
Parking: At Black Point, at Mono Lake County Park, at Lee Vining, at Panum Crater and at Navy Beach.

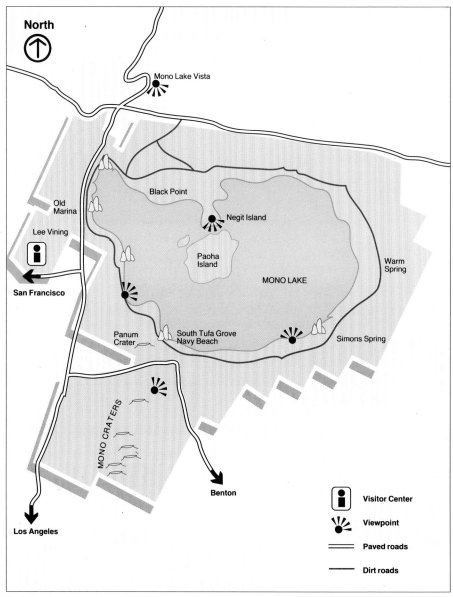

Fuel: Service stations along Inter-state Highway 395 and at Lee Vining.

Roads: In addition to paved roads (Interstate 395, State 167 and 120), there are dirt roads, some negotiable by normal traffic, others by off-road vehicles.

Shops: At Lee Vining.

Accommodation: At Lee Vining and neighbourhood.

Visitor Center: At Lee Vining, it offers permanent exhibitions, audio-visual material and pub-lications on the natural features of the area, plus information. Run by the Mono Lake Committee, it is open throughout the year. For books, maps and information apply also to the Ranger Station at Lee Vining.

Viewpoints: Mono Lake Vista Point along Interstate 395, 19 km (12 miles) north of Lee Vining, and Panum Crater.

Guided tours: Nature trips are organized by the rangers daily in summer and at weekends in the low season; information at the Ranger Station at Lee Vining.

Other activities: There is swim-ming, canoeing and boating; in the period from April to Octo-ber birdwatching is particularly rewarding because of the mi-gration of many species.

more frequently, spelling the end for the Kuzedika who, within a few decades, saw their meager subsistence economy completely destroyed.

Arrival of the aqueducts

Caught up in the fantasies of the gold rushes and the laborious efforts to cultivate the surrounding arid soil, Mono Lake experienced many ups and downs until the fateful year of 1941 when water began to be diverted to feed the Los Angeles aqueduct. Then in 1963 a second aqueduct was built, increasing the amount of water removed. The consequences have been disastrous and the situation continues to worsen. In only forty years the level of the lake has gone down more than 11 m (36 ft), connecting Negit Island with the mainland, and the salinity has doubled. Unless this withdrawal of water is reduced, by the year 2000 the lake's salinity will be trebled and by 2015 quadrupled, making any form of animal life impossible, while Pahoa Island will be transformed into a peninsula. A more prudent policy of water consumption on the part of Los Angeles, aimed at reducing waste to a minimum, would be more than enough to restore to Mono Lake the water needed to raise its level back to normal and preserve the beauty and richness of this natural heritage. It is to be hoped that the impending death of Mono Lake can be averted.

The amazing towers of tufa

Apart from the fact that its very survival is at risk, Mono Lake is famous for the strange tower-like rock formations which line its shores and jut out of the water. Like stalactites and stalagmites, they are made of calcite (calcium carbonate) which, when deposited and crystallized in freshwater environments, form solid mineral masses known as tuff or tufa.

The towers of Mono Lake form around springs, where the calcium dissolved in fresh water combines with the carbonates present in the salt water of the lake, precipitating as calcite: in a sense these formations are underwater fossilized springs, brought to the light by the lowering of lake level.

The tufa therefore also builds up in the sand on the shores and when the water recedes the wind exposes

USEFUL ADVICE

Anyone who visits California, and especially those who have already spent some time in the nearby Sierra Nevada parks of Yosemite, Sequoia and Kings Canyon, should devote at least a few days of their stay to visiting Mono Lake. In summer it is a spectacular place: relaxed bathing and long swims are possible in the lake's salty water, and a variety of interesting trips can be taken among the surrounding mountains and volcanoes.

From October to April thousands of birds, nesting and migrating, throng the shores close to streams and springs, affording a further element of interest, apart from the beauty of the area, for the nature-lover.

As regards clothing, it is wise to protect the head from the hot summer sun with a hat, while a pair of sunglasses will reduce the sometimes troublesome glare of the layers of salt around the lake.

If you take a car, assuming it is not an off-road vehicle, it is best to use only the most solid dirt roads otherwise there is a risk of getting stuck in the soft sand, especially around Mono Lake and at the Mono Craters.

When on foot, always take an abundant supply of water, because it is not easy to come across fresh springs in the highlands surrounding the lake.

For information and advice you can also apply to the staff of the Mono Lake Visitor Center and of the Ranger Station, both situated at Lee Vining. In addition, the Mono Lake Committee, a nonprofit-making association, dedicated to the protection and conservation of the lake and its rich natural and cultural heritage, has published an interesting and detailed monograph entitled *Mono Lake Guidebook*, which can be obtained directly from the Visitor Center or through the mail by application to the Mono Lake Committee/Kutsavi Books, PO Box 29, Lee Vining, California 93541.

CLIMATE

The climate of Mono Lake does not differ very much from that of the Californian Mediterranean type, characterized by rainy winters and hot, dry summers, though it can be rather more arid in this area.

The average annual precipitation is 152–330 mm (6–13 in), hardly sufficient to sustain tree growth. Of this precipitation, 80 per cent falls between November and April, mainly as snow: indeed, fronts from the Pacific Ocean, after crossing the Sierra Nevada, may bury the shores of the lake under 60 cm (2 ft) of snow. On the ensuing cold winter days, a very thick mist, known to the Paiute Indians as *poconip*, will form, coating everything in long crystals of ice. The two intermediate seasons, spring and autumn, are characterized by strong winds which may reach a velocity of 160 kmh (100 mph), while the excessive summer dryness is refreshingly interrupted by violent storms. Overall, the climate of the Mono Lake basin tends to be unpredictable and subject to marked fluctuations, so that in some winters there is exceptional snowfall and in others drought.

it, revealing forms that are even more fantastic; these are the so-called sand tufas.

Both these types of tufa, without equal anywhere in the world, are mineral formations. But are they old? How quickly do they form? And why are those on the northern beaches different from those of the southern beaches? Science is still searching for the answers to these questions. Meanwhile, in order to protect and conserve them effectively, the state of California in 1981 set up the Mono Tufa State Reserve, the boundaries of which coincide with the beach line before 1941.

In 1984 there followed the opening of the first National Park Scenic Area in the United States, with the aim of protecting the natural and cultural resources of the Mono Basin.

WALKS AROUND THE LAKE

There are several short paths in the neighbourhood of Mono Lake (described below), of great interest to nature-lovers; there are information sheets available which draw attention to all the important features.

Black Point   E

A dirt road (follow the signs from Interstate Highway 395) leads to a parking area to the southeast of what appears to be merely a black-coloured hill. It is, in

fact, a volcano that erupted beneath the water of Mono Lake 13,800 years ago.

A marked trail leads to the summit, carved with fissures barely 60–90 cm (2–3 ft) wide and 9–15 m (30–50 ft) deep, the slopes of which are covered with curious white tufaceous masses.

Half a day may be put aside for an interesting and in no way dangerous exploration of the fissures on the southwestern edge of Black Point.

Mono Lake County Park   E

The turning from Interstate Highway 395 to the park is well signposted. This is the ideal place for a picnic, in the shade of poplars which grow alongside a small stream. On the left bank a series of wooden walkways mark the path which leads through meadows (bright with iris in June) to the tufa towers of the northern beach. Like all others, these formations are protected by strict regulations against climbing and removing pieces as souvenirs.

Panum Crater   E

Driving from Lee Vining, leave State Highway 120 by turning left down a dirt road which ends in a parking lot right underneath Panum Crater. The peak, which is reached by a short and easy marked path, is a circular ring of pumice stone, formed after

PICNIC AREAS AND CAMPGROUNDS

There are two official picnic areas equipped with tables and toilet facilities, at the Mono Lake County Park and at South Tufa.

Although there are no campgrounds inside the Scenic Area, many exist in the immediate vicinity: in the Lee Vining Canyon, near the town of that name, in Lundy Canyon, just north of Mono Lake, and along the June Lake Loop, south of the Scenic Area.

Free camping is permitted in some areas outside the Mono Lake Tufa State Reserve. For information and the necessary permit apply to the Ranger Station at Lee Vining.

Panoramic view of Mono Lake, featuring the typical towers of tufa on the shores and on the island.

MONO LAKE, A CONTINENTAL SEA

The Mono Basin forms part of that immense desert region known as the Great Basin, which extends across the states of California, Nevada and Utah from the Sierra Nevada to the Wasatch Mountains. Numerous mountain chains, running north to south, separate more than a hundred desert basins, one of the biggest and most spectacular of which is Death Valley. The Mono Basin is exceptional because it forms a bowl, almost circular in shape, framed by the high, snowcapped peaks of the Sierra Nevada to the west and by the low-lying, desert chains of volcanoes to the north, south and east. At the bottom of the bowl is Mono Lake, fed only by streams which descend from the icy and snowy slopes of the Sierra, since the watercourses that have etched the flanks of the surrounding volcanoes are dry for most of the year. The lake also has no outlets, in common with all the bodies of water that make up the Great Basin, and the rocks on the bottom are non-porous. As a result loss of water comes about only by evaporation caused by wind action and the sun's rays. But this mechanism has an important long-term effect: it leads to a concentration of dissolved mineral salts in the water. In 1981 the salinity of Mono Lake was 9.5 per cent, almost three times that of the sea (3.5 per cent), and for that reason it would be more correct to describe it as an inland or continental sea rather than a lake in the true sense.

From the chemical point of view, the waters of Mono Lake differ markedly from those of the sea and of other salt lakes, as for example Utah's Great Salt Lake, in comparison with which it is poorer in chlorides (19.8 g/l) and richer in sulphates (10.9 g/l) and carbonates (32.7 g/l). Fur-

thermore, because of the high concentration of carbonates, the waters of Mono Lake are strongly basic, with a pH that fluctuates around 10 (bearing in mind that the pH of distilled water is 7 and regarded as neutral, i.e. by definition neither acidic nor basic). The salts present in greatest quantity are sodium chloride, sodium carbonate and sodium sulphate.

How Mono Lake came to assume such characteristics, which make it unique in the world, is a long story covering many millions of years, the last chapter of which has been written by man. The basin originated at about the same time as Death Valley, being related, therefore, to the crustal movements which raised the Sierra Nevada and to the associated volcanic activity. The lake is more recent, although since it dates back millions of years it is one of the oldest on the North American continent. It expanded most rapidly during the Ice Age when it covered a surface of 875 km^2 (338 sq. miles) and measured over 270 m (900 ft) deep (nowadays the average depth is about 15 m (50 ft). Some 12,000 years ago, when the great Quaternary ice-sheets began to retreat, the lake became smaller and shallower until it attained an equilibrium between influx and loss of water. Climatic changes and volcanic activity have gradually lowered or raised the lake level. Eruptions led to the appearance of Negit and Pahoa Islands, respectively 2,000 and less than 325 years ago. Black Point, about 13,800 years old, was also formed by an underwater eruption and is today the only volcano of that type to be completely emergent. Even older, though retaining the characteristic conical shape, are the Mono Craters, which formed around 40,000 years ago.

an explosive eruption around the year 1400. Various marked trails follow the rim of the crater and lead up to the surrounding heights, also volcanic in origin, from where you can admire splendid views.

South Tufa   E

Not far from Panum Crater, this is perhaps the most attractive area. A marked nature trail makes it possible to understand how the tufa towers were formed. Continuing at random along the beach in an easterly direction for about 2.5 km (1½ miles), you reach Navy Beach and the sand tufas.

Longer trips

Among a number of areas which offer a challenge to the expert hiker, two in particular can be tackled in several days (for camping permission apply to the Ranger Station at Lee Vining, where the necessary maps can also be obtained).

Circuit of Mono Lake   M

The ideal point of departure for a walk right around the lake is the town of Lee Vining, situated on an old river delta. There are no roads, paths or tracks, except for a stretch between Old Marina and Navy Beach and the southwestern shore, which makes this tour of the Mono Tufa State Reserve all the more interesting. Observe the regulations and take care along the tracts of muddy beach which you have to follow. Moreover, take a plentiful supply of drinking water.

Mono Craters   D

The chain of the Mono Craters, with twenty volcanic cones which rise 800 m (2,650 ft) above the surrounding territory, afford the chance of some spectacular walks and treks. It is easily reached from the north by State 120 in the direction of Brenton, and from the west by Interstate 395 and several dirt roads which cross the area of the Aeolian Buttes. The lack of trails and springs means that this is terrain only for the more expert trekker.

PHOTOGRAPHIC HINTS

Mono Lake and its surroundings offer excellent opportunities for "lunar" and "fairy-tale" photographs: all you need to do in order to achieve these effects is to choose the right moment from the viewpoint of illumination.

The most photogenic feature is the volcanic island of Pahoa in the center of the lake: its grey contours show up marvellously against the blue of the water's surface. Other interesting pictures can be had by positioning the very curious shapes of the sand tufas (photographs below, opposite and on page 69) in the foreground, and framing them with the mountains of the Sierra Nevada in the background. These rock formations provide splendid subjects just on their own, often creating images reminiscent of the sculptures of the Swiss sculptor Alberto Giacometti.

The most typical and representative features of this environment are undoubtedly the tufa towers, along the edge of the lake; the most promising photographic results can be obtained in late afternoon, standing at right angles to the shadows thrown by each tower, and deriving the maximum benefit from the dramatic contrasts of light and shade.

Similarly in softer light or even after sunset the lake can reveal surprising atmospheric effects, particularly when heightened by a variety of glow and sparkle in the sky; in the absence of the sun you can concentrate creatively on the cooler blue tones of the composition.

A HABITAT SWARMING WITH LIFE

The chemical characteristics of the waters may encourage the assumption that Mono Lake is an environment with little or no plant or animal life, or at best colonized by a few microscopic organisms. The truth is, however, that a simple yet effective food chain makes it an ecosystem that swarms with life (as in all difficult environments a few species are represented here by an enormous number of individuals), with particular emphasis on water birds.

Microscopic algae trap solar energy by photosynthesis; and small anostracan crustaceans of the genus *Artemia*, as well as larvae of brine shrimps and brine flies, feed on the algae and are in turn consumed by birds. The cycle is brought full circle by the algae, the *Artemia* crustaceans, the fly larvae and the birds which, when they die and fall to the bottom of the lake, are duly decomposed by the action of bacteria; the detritus which forms fertilizes the algae and in this way the entire cycle begins again.

The birds are not present all year round along the shores of Mono Lake because the populations of invertebrates on which they feed undergo marked seasonal fluctuations. It happens, in fact, that in summer the water of the lake, heated up by the sun, is separated into two distinct layers: the upper part is warm, highly oxygenated and full of crustaceans and dead algae; the lower section, on the other hand, is colder, contains little oxygen and is populated only by algae. In winter this system of layers no longer applies, the different depths of water intermingle and the algae are still there in abundance, while the adult crustaceans die; only the eggs they have laid in the autumn

survive, miniscule cysts which are capable of overwintering without coming to harm. In this cold season, because their principal food source is absent, birds abandon Mono Lake and only return with the thaw.

A study of the birds has revealed the presence of ninety-eight aquatic species (the full list can be found in the *Mono Lake Guidebook*), and for five of these the lake is of enormous importance. The California gull (*Larus californicus*) and the snowy (or Kentish) plover (*Charadrius alexandrinus*), which nest there, Wilson's phalarope (*Phalaropus tricolor*), the northern phalarope (*P. lobatus*) and the blacknecked grebe (*Podiceps nigricollis*), which frequent it during their migrations. Hundreds of thousands of birds are also attracted to Mono Lake by the fact that it constitutes an abundant source of food entirely at their disposal. Indeed, in contrast to what happens in other lakes, the complete absence of fish in these waters means that they encounter no competition.

However, the many grave problems which for years have threatened the lake cannot help but have adverse repercussions on the local birdlife. In 1979 Negit Island, as a result of further lowering of the water level, was linked to the beach by a narrow strip of dry land. This circumstance was quickly exploited by coyotes who chased away some 33,000 nesting California gulls and preyed on their eggs and chicks.

Since then, although the island has been artificially isolated and carefully protected, the gulls have failed to nest along the lake, and the result has been a disastrous drop in the numbers of chicks raised each year: from an average of 26,800 (65 per cent on Negit Island) before 1979 to a mere 5,000 or so in 1984.

CALIFORNIA

KINGS CANYON AND SEQUOIA
NATIONAL PARKS

The Sierra Nevada is a chain of high mountains, extending for about 400 km (250 miles) from north to south, wholly within the state of California. The highest snowcapped peaks, which inspired the Spaniards to give the range that name ("snowy mountain chain"), are situated in the southern sector and culminate in Mount Whitney, which at 4,418 m (14,491 ft) is the highest mountain in the United States, excluding Alaska. A vast portion of the mountain region around Mount Whitney, extending for about one quarter the length of the entire state, is occupied by the two adjoining National Parks of Sequoia and Kings Canyon. The areas, which geographically are continuous and exhibit the same natural features, constitute a single entity and are administered as such, although, historically, they were established at different times. Sequoia was proclaimed a National Park on 25 September 1890 and is the oldest of California's five parks, having preceded Yosemite by a mere five days. Kings Canyon is much younger, established 50 years afterwards.

Address: Superintendent, Sequoia and Kings Canyon National Parks, Three Rivers, California 93271, tel. (209) 565-3341.
Area: Sequoia, 1,630 km² (630 sq. miles); Kings Canyon, 1,850 km² (715 sq. miles).
Altitude: Sequoia, 520–4,418 m (1,705–14,491 ft); Kings Canyon, 1,400–4,340 m (4,592–14,235 ft).
Access: Sequoia, from the west by State Highway 198; Kings Canyon, from the west of State Highway 180. Both parks accessible from the east on foot.
Opening times: Sequoia, all year round, 24 hours a day; Kings Canyon, Grant Grove throughout the year, 24 hours a day, Cedar Grove May–October.

The names of different origin

Sequoia National Park derives its name from the sequoias which grow within it, and which were so called in honour of the Cherokee chief Sequoyah (1760–1843). The Cherokees invented an alphabet of eighty-six characters and taught their tribes to read and write. This so much impressed the Austrian botanist who first classified these giant trees that he named them *Sequoia gigantea* (the correct modern scientific name is *Sequoiadendron giganteum*).

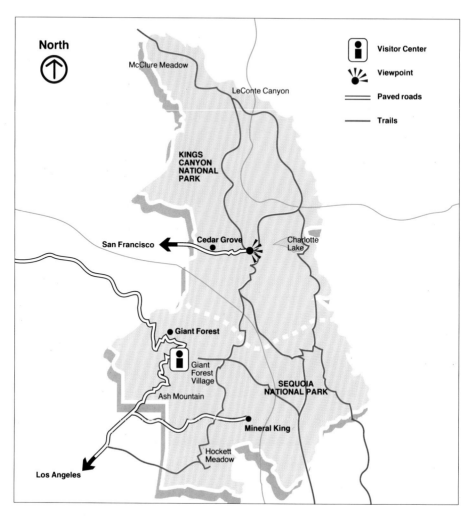

Entry charge: $5 for cars, entry free with Golden Eagle Passport. **Fuel:** At Grant Grove Village, at Cedar Grove Village, at Lodgepole and at Three Rivers. **Roads:** State Highways 180 and 198 are open throughout the year, except for a short stretch which links Grant Grove and Cedar Grove, open only in summer. A paved road, open all year round, the Generals Highway, links the two parks, 74 km (46 miles) from the Ash Mountain entrance to Grant Grove. In Sequoia there are also three dirt roads (Crystal Cave, Mineral King and South Fork), closed in winter.

Shops: At Grant Grove Village, at Giant Forest Village and at Three Rivers; at Cedar Grove Village and Lodgepole in summer. **Accommodation:** At Giant Forest (motel and cabins), at Grant Grove Village and at Cedar Grove Village. For information and advance booking write to or telephone Sequoia and Kings Canyon Guest Services, Sequoia National Park, California 93262, tel. (209) 561-3314; and Wilsonia Lodge, Kings Canyon National Park, California 93633, tel. (209) 335-2310.

Visitor Center: Sequoia, near the Ash Mountain entrance and at

Lodgepole; Kings Canyon, at Grant Grove and at Cedar Grove. They are open from 8 am to 5 pm. **Guided tours:** Daily nature trips in summer and treks with snowshoes at weekends during the winter. Apply to the Visitor Centers for detailed programmes. **Other activities:** Horse riding, fishing (license obligatory), cross-country skiing, ski-mountaineering and rock climbing. **Beware of:** Sudden changes in weather at high altitude; falling rocks, exposed paths and drops. **Facilities for the disabled:** There are no architectural obstacles in most buildings and facility areas.

The origin of the name Kings Canyon is rather more complex. A certain Gabriel Moraga, an explorer with the Spanish army, discovered a new river on 6 January 1806 and in memory of that day, the Epiphany, named it El Rio de los Santos Reyes, i.e. "the river of the Magi Kings." Once anglicized, the name was abbreviated to Kings River, and the valley hewn out by the waters of the river's southern branch (South Fork) was called Kings Canyon.

An unexplored region

Until 1864 this long tract of the Sierra Nevada was unknown, at least to the white man. Yet the western slopes, which descend gently towards the broad San Joaquin Valley, were in fact colonized between the years 1000 and 1500 by a group of Indians – the Monachi or Monos – who came from the Great Basin which extends east to the Sierra Nevada. The Spaniards and then the Mexicans never pushed into the interior of the Sierra, so that the Monos continued living there undisturbed, occupying low-lying terrain in winter and moving higher in summer when they established communications with the tribes inhabiting areas beyond the mountains. For this purpose they used the trail which follows Kings Canyon, climbs Bubbs Creek, crosses the Kearsarge Pass (3,603 m/11,818 ft) and descends towards Owens Valley, as indicated by various archaeological finds.

With the annexation of California by the United States and the successive waves of the gold rush, Americans, too, began to travel through the Sierra Nevada. They were mostly prospectors, hunters and adventurers, who never had any relish for rough places and made no attempt to probe more deeply into the mountains. In contrast, a group of scientists working for the State Geological Service organized an expedition in 1864 to map the unexplored territories of the Sierra and, taking the trail of the Monos, eventually found themselves among the high, snow-capped peaks. One of these was Mount Whitney, named after the expedition's leader.

Thus began a new chapter in the history of this wild region, which was to become a battleground for those Americans who banded together to protect the nation's natural heritage and those who were equally determined, come what may, to exploit it.

USEFUL ADVICE

There are limitations to the trips that can be made in these parks because of both natural and human factors. Due to the climatic and environmental conditions, the high-altitude routes are accessible only in the summer months, which also include September. The latter relate to restrictions imposed by the park authorities to control the number of people on certain tourist trails, the reason being that the sheer pressure of human traffic along these routes threatens to cause irreparable damage to the fragile high-mountain environments. To walk these particular trails it is therefore necessary to have a permit, which can be obtained free of charge from the Visitor Centers or by mail. Advance bookings for the summer season only open on 1 March and should be made at least seven days before undertaking the trip; apply to the Superintendent for the appropriate form if booking in writing. Permits are issued daily on the spot until they run out, so it is best to apply early in the morning to avoid having to change your route or wait until the following day to do the trip. There are also some areas which are subject to special regulations regarding the activities allowed there (camping, etc.).

Particular care should be paid to not leaving foodstuffs around because of the presence of bears. Finally, some advice on clothing: the climate in high mountains can vary immensely, so it is important to be prepared for the onset of cold, damp weather despite the apparent conditions at the time of departure. Take along additional layers to keep warm (sweater, windcheater, woolly cap, gloves, etc.).

CLIMATE

The vast region occupied by the two parks, though predominantly alpine, is not climatically homogeneous: between the peak of Mount Whitney and the low, hilly western slopes of the Sierra there is, in fact, a height difference of some 4,000 m (13,120 ft). Lower down the climate is markedly two-seasonal: from May to October there is very little rain and temperatures are high, while from November to April the climate is milder, but never cold, and very rainy. The contour line of 1,400 m (4,600 ft), above which precipitations take the form of snow in winter, represents the lower level of the conifer forests which continue to a height of about 2,700 m (7,560 ft). The climate of this belt, in which all the parks' tourist attractions are situated, varies according to the four seasons: little rain in summer, snow in winter and intermediate conditions in spring and autumn. At higher altitudes the climate becomes decidedly sub-arctic, with a very short summer and many months of frost.

Bitter fights for the parks

In the forefront of these battles was the important naturalist and environmentalist John Muir, who in the course of his solitary travels late in the nineteenth century was so attracted to these mountains that he founded the famous Sierra Club, which still functions to this day. His efforts, together with those of other conservationists of the time, led almost immediately to the establishment of the Sequoia but not the Kings Canyon National Park, despite the fact that similar dangers threatened both areas: reckless cutting down of the sequoias, overgrazing, mineral activity, etc. Since then Sequoia has been extended several times, and today, along with the adjacent Kings Canyon, it covers an area of almost 3,500 km² (1,350 sq. miles), which safeguards the natural resources of one of the most beautiful mountain ranges in the world.

KINGS CANYON NATIONAL PARK

Marked trails

The trails of the two supervised areas of the park are different in character; those of Grant Grove are short

and easy, whereas those of Cedar Grove are more arduous and provide access to treks at high altitude. The length and time given apply to the outward and return journeys, unless otherwise specified.

GRANT GROVE

Only the most important trails are described here. Many of the trips can be combined.

North Grove Loop Trail   E

2.4 km (1½ miles), 1 hour 10 minutes

Begins and ends at the General Grant Tree car park; short, simple, circular walk which follows an old dirt road through a wood of giant sequoias, sugar pines (*Pinus lambertiana*) and white firs (*Abies concolor*).

Dead Giant Loop Trail   E

3.5 km (2¼ miles), 120 m (394 ft) change in elevation, 1½ hours

Begins and ends at the General Grant Tree car park. Easy walk which brings you to the Dead Giant, a gigantic sequoia which fell a few years ago, and to a viewpoint over Sequoia Lake.

The Sequoia National Park is the home of the big trees or giant sequoias, famous throughout the world as the largest of all trees in bulk, although the related redwoods grow taller. Thousands of years ago much of the northern hemisphere was covered by forests of giant sequoias; nowadays, however, they remain only on the western slope of the Sierra Nevada.

On pages 76 and 77: Kings Canyon extends to the north of the Sequoia National Park and, like the latter, its eastern section is characterized by wild and beautiful mountain scenery. Steep walls and crags provide spectacular panoramas. From Cedar Grove, in the center of the park, tourists can walk the miles and miles of trails in all directions.

This trail is also linked to another circular trail of 9.5 km (6 miles) which brings you into sight of the lower section of Kings Canyon.

General Grant Tree Trail　　　　　　E

3.7 km (2¼ miles), 1½ hours

Beginning and ending at the Visitor Center, this is the most popular trail in the park. It provides an easy path across the Azalea Campground, the Columbine picnic area and around the huge General Grant sequoia. At the Visitor Center you can listen to a recorded tape with a 30-minute commentary on the trees you will see along the trail.

Manzanita Trail　　　　　　　　　　E

5.3 km (3¼ miles), 250 m (820 ft) change in elevation, 2 hours

This attractive circular trail begins and ends at the Visitor Center. The path climbs Manzanita Hill and reaches the crest of the Park Ridge where it joins the Park Ridge Trail. From here it leads down via the Azalea Trail (so called because of the numerous azaleas which grow there), crosses Wilsonia Road and returns to the Visitor Center.

Park Ridge Trail　　　　　　　　　　E

7.5 km (4¾ miles), 60 m (197 ft) change in elevation, 3 hours

This easy trail, with fine views, begins and ends at Panoramic Point. It runs almost entirely along the crest, from which you can see Hume Lake in the adjacent Sequoia National Forest and, farther east, the San Joaquin Valley. On a clear day you can also see as far as the mountains of the Coast Range, over 160 km (100 miles) away. The trail ends at the fire tower, operative from May to October; it is possible to acquire a permit to climb it.

Sunset Trail　　　　　　　　　　　　M

9.6 km (6 miles), 400 m (1,312 ft) change in elevation, 3/4 hours

Begins at the Visitor Center, ends at Sequoia Lake. This is the most tiring but also the most rewarding of the trails in the Grant Grove area. Along the route

PICNIC AREAS AND CAMPGROUNDS

The picnic areas with facilities are strung out along the main roads to coincide with the principal tourist sights. The campgrounds are situated in various surroundings, from the eastern slopes of the hills covered with chaparral to the conifer forests, at altitudes that range from 640 m (2,100 ft) to 2,300 m (7,545 ft). Lodgepole, Grant Grove and Atwell lie close to the sequoia woods. All are open in summer but only a few in spring, and then without running water. From 14 June to 14 September stays are restricted to 14 days. At Lodgepole advance booking is possible from mid May to mid September (apply to Ticketron, Dept. R, Hackensack Ave., Hackensack, NJ 07601).

Grant Grove: Sunset (184 places, $6 per night, open only in summer), Azalea (118 places, $6 per night, open all year), Crystal Springs (67 places, $6 per night, open only in summer).

Cedar Grove: Sheep Creek (111 places), Moraine (120 places), Sentinel (83 places); $6 per night, open May to October, altitude 1,400 m (4,592 ft).

Sequoia (low altitude): Potwisha (44 places, $6 per night, altitude 640 m/2,100 ft, open all year), Buckeye Flat (28 places, $6 per night, altitude 850 m/2,788 ft, open mid April to mid October, no trailers), South Fork (13 places, $4 per night, altitude 1,110 m/3,641 ft, open all year, no trailers).

Giant Forest: Lodgepole (260 places, $8 per night from May to mid September, $6 at other periods, open all year, altitude 2,050 m/6,724 ft).

Mineral King: Cold Springs (37 places, altitude 2,290 m/7,511 ft), Atwell Mill (23 places, altitude 2,025 m/6,642 ft); $4 per night, open in summer, no trailers.

There is in addition the facility area of Stony Creek and free camping is allowed with a permit.

are two beautiful waterfalls: Viola Falls and Ella Falls. The trail, about 2 km (1¼ miles) from the start, crosses the South Boundary Trail.

CEDAR GROVE

Roaring River Falls Trail   E

1.6 km (1 mile), 45 minutes

Begins at the Roaring River Falls car park; end at the falls of the same name. Easy walk on a trail of level ground which leads to the Roaring River Falls.

Zumwalt Meadow Trail   E

2.4 km (1½ miles), 1½ hours

Begins and ends at the Zumwalt Meadow car park. Short walk on the flat which leads along the banks of Kings River, through fields and woods.

Hotel Creek Trail   M

8.8 km (5½ miles), 370 m (1,214 ft) change in elevation, 4 hours

Begins at the main road 400 m (440 yds) before the riding stables; ends at a viewpoint overlooking the Cedar Grove valley. This trail climbs a small lateral valley, here containing Hotel Creek, a tributary of the Kings River. After only 200 m (220 yds) it passes the Hotel Creek waterfall, beyond which the path begins to ascend the side of the canyon in a succession of sharp turns. At the top there is a splendid view of the canyon beneath.

Don Cecil Trail   M

19.6 km (12¼ miles), 1,200 m (3,936 ft) change in elevation, 8 hours

Begins at the main road 400 m (440 yds) beyond the entrance to the Sentinel Campground; ends on Lookout Peak (2,600 m/8,528 ft). A trip to the summit of the western boundary of the park. From the top there is a good view north to the Monarch Divide, a long series of peaks that rise to over 3,300 m (10,825 ft) which form the watershed between the Middle and South Forks of the Kings River.

Mist Falls/Paradise Valley Trail   M

12.8/22.5 km (8/14 miles), 180/450 m (590/1,509 ft) change in elevation, 6/12 hours

Begins at Roads End; ends at Mist Falls or at Paradise Valley (the distance, change in elevation and time refer respectively to the first and second destinations). This trail is one of the most popular in the park and there are many walkers in summer. After the first 3.2 km (2 miles) it arrives at a junction: the right-hand track leads to the valley of Sphinx Creek, while the main path proceeds towards Mist Falls, which is reached after about 3 km (1¾ miles) or 6 km (3¾ miles) from the departure point. From there the trail becomes easier going and eventually reaches the flat Paradise Valley. You can then continue along Woods Creek to the junction with the John Muir Trail.

Copper Creek Trail   M

28 km (17½ miles), 1,730 m (5,674 ft) change in elevation, 2 days

Begins at Roads End; ends at Granite Pass (3,253 m/11,555 ft). This long and tiring trail leads to Granite Pass, the entrance proper to the northernmost sector of the park. Before reaching the pass, the trail runs past the Granite Lakes.

SEQUOIA NATIONAL PARK

Marked Trails

As in Kings Canyon, there are hundreds of kilometers of marked trails to be found in Sequoia National Park – altogether 1,190 km (744 miles) between the two parks. The less demanding trails, taking up a single day and thus 8/10 hours of walking, are to be found in the two best developed tourist areas: Giant Forest and Mineral King.

GIANT FOREST

In this area of about 13 km² (5 sq. miles) there are trails covering a total of 65 km (40½ miles), which run through the finest, most majestic sequoia forest in the world. To avoid going wrong, pay careful attention to the colour of the signs.

PHOTOGRAPHIC HINTS

The huge sequoias are marvellous subjects for photography but the first rule is to avoid taking pictures of groups of them because the unvarying mass of greenery is unlikely to give good results. It is far better to concentrate on details of the surroundings and of individual trees. Photographs of the underwood taken from within the trees will avoid the problem of strong contrasting areas of bright sunlight and forest darkness for which the film may not be able to compensate. You can get very interesting results, too, by taking part shots and close-ups of the sequoias, focusing on the lines and patterns of branches and trunks. Looking especially for colour effects and the interplay of light and shade on the dark structure can be a marvellous exercise in studying detail. An example is the photograph on the left which, using a 200 mm lens, manages to compress three elements into perspective, so that subjects located several meters from one another appear on a single plane, the graphic effect of the picture accentuated by the parallel lines.

Kings Canyon and Cedar Grove present few problems for photography. The most interesting colour effects are to be had in autumn, but with due patience and imagination opportunities will be found for excellent pictures at other seasons as well. Take your shots of canyon walls when they are still well illuminated by daylight, otherwise the pictures will turn out hopelessly dark and empty of detail. As a rule, the trunks of uprooted trees and the roots themselves, weathered by the sun and storms, take on a subtle range of orange tones around sunset. With back-lighting, during the late afternoon, the sweep of mountain peaks, taken with a 200 mm lens, will provide spectacular compositions.

THE RED GIANT: THE SEQUOIA

The giant sequoia (*Sequoiadendron giganteum*) is a conifer of the family Taxodiaceae, also known as the big tree because of its enormous dimensions. The tallest specimen, known as the General Sherman tree, in Giant Forest, stands 83.7 m (274 ft), but the notable feature of this tree is not its height. In fact, a related species, the redwood (*Sequoia sempervirens*), which grows in the coastal mountains of northern California, normally measures more than 100 m (330 ft) high, probably benefiting from the moister oceanic climate. The giant sequoia, however, has a much bigger trunk: the base circumference of the General Sherman tree is no less than 31.2 m (102 ft). Moreover these trees reach a remarkable age, the oldest of them being around 3,000 years. The giant sequoia also has other distinctive characteristics which deserve brief mention. The trunk is covered with very thick bark, deeply fissured and red in colour, which contrasts sharply with the green of the needle-like leaves, only 5-6 mm (¼ in) long, borne on large branches which form a fairly sparse cylindrical dome high above the ground. The cones have the shape and size of a hen's egg and contain about 150-250 seeds. Each year, a medium-sized tree produces on average 2,000 new cones which, in addition to those of the preceding year, bring the number of cones to be found at the same time on the same tree to about 15,000. The seeds fall to the ground when the cone is ripe or, more frequently, because an animal is at work: one squirrel was seen to cause 538 cones to fall within a mere 31 minutes. Of all the seeds produced by a tree, 98 per cent will not germinate, for various reasons; of the remaining 2 per cent, the only plantlets to thrive and develop are those which find favourable surrounding conditions: soil rich in nutrients, reduced competition for light, etc. A highly important role in the creation of such positive conditions is played by fire; the

adult sequoias, thanks to the protection afforded them by their thick and almost fireproof bark, are not harmed by conflagrations which, in turn, leave open spaces free of other undergrowth, thus enabling new plantlets to receive all the light necessary for their growth (photograph below).

The giant sequoia is able to reach such enormous dimensions thanks to two special attributes: 1) the very extensive and shallow root apparatus (a root may appear up to 30 m/100 ft from the trunk but never probe to a depth of more than 1 m/3¼ ft), which gives the long, massive trunk considerable stability; 2) the lightness of the wood (specific weight 55.8 g/c.c. – about one-fifth that of oak wood), which enables a large mass to develop.

Today the giant sequoia grows only in a belt of the western slope of the Sierra Nevada about 400 km (250 miles) long and at an altitude of 1,500–2,100 m (4,920–6,890 ft); it is a very small area in comparison with the wide distribution that sequoias enjoyed some 70 million years ago when they grew at medium latitudes in Europe, Asia and North America, as is documented by numerous finds of fossil leaves and cones. Within the present area, the giant sequoia is always found in association with other conifers, avoiding the zones inside the canyons in preference for flat ridges where they form characteristic groves.

The largest specimens have curiously been given the names of famous men in American history; the four biggest, among the thousands proudly conserved in the two parks, are the General Sherman, General Grant, Frank E. Boole and Hart Trees. They are actually not necessarily the most beautiful but each tree has its own particular charm and for this reason, in addition to their scientific value, they deserve to be protected together in this, their last natural environment.

Hazelwood Nature Trail   E

1.6 km (1 mile), 1½ hours

Begins and ends at Generals Highway, opposite the Giant Forest Lodge. An easy, circular walk on level ground through sequoia woods; numerous explanatory plaques give concise historical information. Follow the purple signs.

Crescent Meadow and Log Meadow Trail   E

2.9 km (1¾ miles), 2 hours

Begins and ends at the Crescent Meadow car park. Circular trail which goes along the side of the two meadows concerned; the oldest pioneers' cabin in the park can be found on this trail. Follow the orange signs; the first part coincides with the High Sierra Trail.

Congress Trail   E

3.2 km (2 miles), 2 hours

Begins and ends at the General Sherman Tree. This circular trail goes through part of the Alta Plateau, a section of the Giant Forest where various sequoias with important names to them grow. In addition to the General Sherman and the General Lee, there are sequoias named after Lincoln, McKinley, Chief Sequoyah, etc. An illustrated guide is sold at the beginning of the trail. Follow the yellow signs.

Tokopah Falls Trail   E

6.4 km (4 miles), 3½ hours

Begins at the Lodgepole campground and ends at Tokopah Falls. This is an easy trail which runs along the Marble Fork of the Kaweah River to the falls of the Tokopah Valley between high granite walls.

Moro Rock and Soldiers Trail Loop   E

7.4 km (4½ miles), 70 m (230 ft) change in elevation, 3¾ hours

Begins and ends at Giant Forest Village, just west of the cafeteria. This trail constitutes an easy climb to the top of Moro Rock (2,050 m/6,724 ft), from where there is a splendid view of the western slopes of the Sierra and the San Joaquin Valley as far as the distant

Coast Range. The face of Moro Rock opposite the one ascended by the trail is a spectacular granite wall 100 m (330 ft) high. The entire trail is signposted in red.

Huckleberry Meadow Loop Trail   E

8 km (5 miles), 4 hours

Begins and ends at Generals Highway, opposite Giant Forest Lodge. This circular trail leads to the heart of the Giant Forest and is one of those less frequented. Of particular interest are the picturesque meadow after which the trail is named and several gigantic sequoias about 90 m (295 ft) high, including the Washington Tree.

Sequoias Trail and Circle Meadow Loop   E

9.6 km (6 miles), 4 hours

Begins and ends at the General Sherman Tree. The trail is not difficult but slightly tiring (moderately steep stretches) across the eastern part of the Giant Forest, featuring some of the finest sequoia woods in the park.

Alta Trail   M

21.5 km (13½ miles), 1,200 m (3,936 ft) change in elevation, 2 days

Begins in the area of the Wolverton car park; ends on the summit of Alta Peak (3,414 m/11,198 ft). From here there is a superb panoramic view of the Kaweah Basin, the Great Western Divide and Mount Whitney. There are camping sites along the route.

Pear Lake Trail   M

21.5 km (13½ miles), 700 m (2,296 ft) change in elevation, 2 days

Begins and ends in the area of the Wolverton car park; ends at Pear Lake (2,898 m/9,505 ft). About 3.2 km (2 miles) from the start, the path divides: the left fork (Watchtower Trail) is longer but less strenuous, the right fork (Hump Trail) shorter but steeper.

On pages 84 and 85: in order to accentuate the outline and structure of this young sequoia, back-lighting has been used to bring out the shape of the foliage.

Twin Lakes   M

22.5 km (14 miles), 860 m (2,821 ft) change in elevation, 2 days

Begins at the Lodgepole campground; ends at Twin Lakes (2,895 m/9,496 ft). The trail flanks a number of alpine meadows, the loveliest of which is Cahoon Meadow (not marked on maps). Twin Lakes lies at the foot of the Silliman Pass (3,169 m/10,394 ft).

MINERAL KING

The rocks of Kings Canyon are excellent subjects for photography, especially when they take on these warm tones at sunset. The quality of pictures is naturally heightened by the clear atmosphere at high altitude.

This area only relatively recently became part of the Sequoia National Park in 1978, having been an area of mineral activity and the subject of a plan for

conversion into a winter sports tourist center, fortunately rejected. The name of this small, high-altitude valley – the bottom of the valley is about 2,300 m (7,544 ft) above sea level – was given to it by those who believed, between 1870 and 1880, that they had discovered deposits of silver as vast as those in Nevada. Such hopes soon faded and extraction operations were terminated.

The trails of this zone, described in detail in a pamphlet distributed at the Visitor Center, are fairly strenuous given the altitude and steepness of the valley slopes, but they lead to a number of lakes which make the effort worthwhile. Some of them are described below: the distances and times required comprise the outward and return trips.

On pages 88 and 89: macrophotographs using a telephoto lens, such as this one of the bark of a sequoia, are very successful at capturing the play of light and shade on the irregular surfaces of the forest.

Timber Gap Trail   M

6.5 km (4 miles), 430 m (1,410 ft) change in elevation, 3 hours

Begins at the Sawtooth-Monarch car park; ends at Timber Gap (2,880 m/9,446 ft). This trail follows an old, steep miners' road through a dense forest of firs. Once you arrive at the panoramic pass, Timber Gap, which is the highlight of the excursion, the path continues towards the valley of the Middle Fork Kaweah River through the central region of the park.

Eagle Lake Trail   M

11 km (7 miles), 670 m (2,198 ft) change in elevation, 5 hours

Begins at the Eagle-Mosquito car park; ends at Eagle Lake. The first 1,600 m (1 mile) coincide with another trail, the White Chief Trail, then the path bends right towards Eagle Canyon, which is bright with flowers in early summer. Eagle Lake is a magnificent example of an alpine lake of glacial origin, surrounded by high rock crags. An interesting point along the trail is the sinkhole into which the waters of Eagle Creek vanish; nobody has so far been able to discover the stream's subterranean course.

Monarch Lakes Trail   M

14.4 km (9 miles), 785 m (2,575 ft) change in elevation, 6 hours

Begins at the Sawtooth-Monarch car park; ends at the Monarch Lakes (3,235 m/10,611 ft). The initial stretch of the trail coincides with the Timber Gap Trail. The path then follows two lakes in the direction of Lost Canyon and Kern Canyon, over the Sawtooth Pass (3,536 m/11,598 ft).

Crystal Lake Trail   M

15.8 km (10 miles), 915 m (3,001 ft) change in elevation, 7 hours

Begins at the Sawtooth-Monarch car park; ends at Crystal Lake (3,365 m/11,037 ft). For a long stretch the trail coincides with the Monarch Lakes Trail. It branches off about 5 km (3 miles) from the start (turn right at the junction).

Franklin Lake Trail   M

17.4 km (11 miles), 770 m (2,526 ft) change in elevation, 7 hours

Begins at the Eagle-Mosquito car park; ends at Franklin Lake (3,147 m/10,322 ft). The trail follows an old miners' road, after passing on the left the fork to Franklin Pass (3,566 m/11,696 ft), and ascends to Farewell Gap (3,227 m/10,585 ft). The lake lies beyond the pass, across Franklin Creek.

LOW-ALTITUDE TRAILS

The trails described briefly below are all at low altitude, through low-lying hilly areas covered with chaparral. They are very peaceful and of great interest to the nature-lover.

Middle Fork Trail   M

14.5 km (9 miles), 370 m (1,214 ft) change in elevation, 6½ hours

Begins near the Buckeye Flat campground; ends at the confluence of Panther Creek and Middle Fork. From here it is possible to go on to Mehrten Creek, 200 m (220 yds) higher up. There are free camping areas at Panther Creek and Mehrten Creek.

Lady Bug Camp   E

6.4 km (4 miles), 230 m (754 ft) change in elevation, 2½ hours

Begins at the South Fork campground; ends at Lady Bug Camp. From here the trail continues for 2.4 km (1½ miles) to Whiskey Log Camp, 200 m (220 yds) higher up.

Garfield Grove Trail   M

6.4 km (4 miles) outward only, 820 m (269 ft) change in elevation, 4 hours

Begins at the South Fork campground; ends in a grove of giant sequoias. An arduous trail.

MOUNT WHITNEY

A dense network of trails, some at considerable heights, crisscrosses the High Sierra, the high-altitude region of the Sierra Nevada, and quite a number run through the Sequoia and Kings Canyon areas. Many of the longer trails are so frequented, both on foot and on horseback, that they are subject to a control on numbers; the most famous of these, and with good reason, are the John Muir Trail, which begins in Yosemite Valley and ends at Whitney Portal, on the eastern slopes of Mount Whitney (right), the High Sierra Trail, which is wholly located in the Sequoia National Park, crossing it from west to east, and the Rae Lakes Trail, which starts and terminates at Roads Ends. The ascent of Mount Whitney (4,418 m/14,491 ft) comes into a separate category. Climbers armed with suitable maps can choose from a variety of routes, but it is essential to consult the rangers as to the condition of the paths to be taken.

The ascent of Mount Whitney is a long trip but presents no particular climbing difficulties, so much so that you can even get to the top with mules. The closest point to the summit that can be reached by car is Whitney Portal, situated on the eastern face of the mountain, just outside the bounds of the Sequoia National Park, at an altitude of 2,550 m (8,364 ft). A paved road, open to traffic only in the summer, links it with the town of Lone Pine in the Owens Valley.

CALIFORNIA

YOSEMITE
NATIONAL PARK

The Yosemite National Park is certainly one of the most internationally famous parks and also one of the loveliest: it is visited every year by over 2.5 million people from all over the world. Within its boundaries lies the heart of the Sierra Nevada, with its impressive granite peaks, vast forests, meadows, lakes and waterfalls. Everything blends perfectly to create an almost magical sense of harmony, undisturbed by the possible harshness of mountain heights.

The "grassy valley"

It was probably more than 4,000 years ago that the first men entered this region. In the ensuing centuries they were followed by other Indian people, including a tribe that called the Yosemite Valley "Ahwahnee," which, roughly translated, means the "grassy valley." They then called themselves the "Ahwahneechee."

The lives of these Indian hunters and food gatherers were not disturbed until the middle of the nineteenth century, when the area began to attract hordes of gold prospectors.

Coexistence was from the start far from peaceful, and in the spring of 1851 the whites banded together in an armed contingent, the Mariposa Battalion, in order to capture as many Indians as possible and herd them into a reserve. The expedition failed because the Indians easily managed to elude the soldiers and to hide, but the enthusiastic descriptions of the beauties of the valley which the whites brought back on their return was to bring about irreversible change to the place and its inhabitants.

Address: Superintendent, PO Box 577, Yosemite National Park, California 95389, tel. (209) 372-0200.
Area: 3,078 km² (1,189 sq. miles).
Altitude: From 610 m (2,000 ft) to 3,997 m (13,110 ft) above sea level.
Access: From west by State Highways 120, 140 and 41; from east only by State Highway 120.
Opening times: All year round.
Entry charge: $5 per vehicle; 50 cents per person in a bus, on foot, horseback or bicycle.
Parking: In Yosemite Valley and at Mariposa Grove; at Glacier Point, Wawona, Crane Flat and Tuolumne Meadow only in summer.

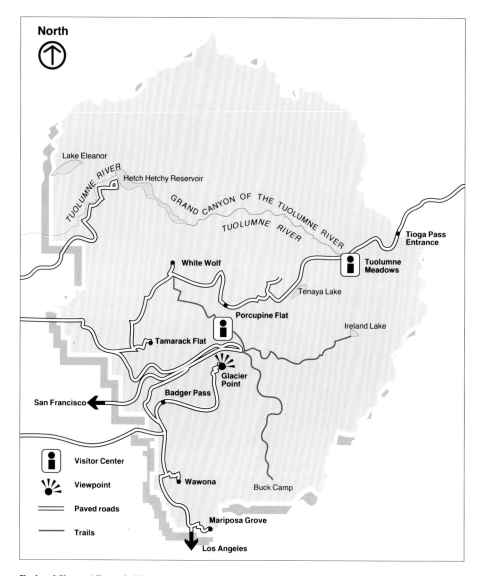

North

Lake Eleanor

Hetch Hetchy Reservoir

TUOLUMNE RIVER

GRAND CANYON OF THE TUOLUMNE RIVER

TUOLUMNE RIVER

Tioga Pass Entrance

White Wolf

Tuolumne Meadows

Tenaya Lake

Porcupine Flat

Ireland Lake

Tamarack Flat

Glacier Point

Badger Pass

San Francisco

Visitor Center

Viewpoint

Paved roads

Trails

Wawona

Buck Camp

Mariposa Grove

Los Angeles

Fuel and Shops: All year in Yosemite Valley and at Wawona; the service stations along the Tioga Road are open only in summer. **Roads:** State Highways 140 and 41 are open throughout the year, while the stretch of State 120 which crosses the park, called Tioga Road, is closed in winter. **Accommodation:** Many possibilities in Yosemite Valley, at Wawona, Tuolumne Meadow and White Wolf. For information and advance booking apply to Yosemite Park and Curry Company reservations, 5410 East Home, Fresno, California 93727, tel. (209) 252-4848. **Visitor Center:** The Visitor Centers of Yosemite Valley and Tuolumne Meadow (latter open only in summer) offer information and publications. Permits and information are also supplied by all the rangers' stations. **Museums:** Happy Isles Nature Center and Indian Cultural Museum in Yosemite Valley; Sequoia Ecology Museum at Mariposa Grove. **Guided tours:** The Visitors Centers provide programmes on trips guided by park naturalists. **Other activities:** Horse and bicycle riding, swimming, fishing (with license), skiing (in winter) and rock climbing. **Facilities for disabled:** no architectural obstacles in most buildings; certain trails equipped; activities and material specifically for the deaf, dumb and blind.

Establishment of the National Park

Within only a few years, in 1864, serious problems of environmental degradation (overgrazing, etc.) as a result of the increase in human presence were already being recorded, and it soon became evident that official intervention would be necessary without delay, to safeguard and conserve the natural heritage. As a result, thanks above all to the efforts of John Muir, first president of the Sierra Club (an environmental association that is still active today), the National Park was founded in 1890.

Marked trails

More than 1,200 km (750 miles) of trails have been marked out in the park; some cover simple, short walks, others constitute treks that are both strenuous and of long duration; between them they offer everyone the chance to appreciate the natural beauties of the place at the pace they choose (many trails are also accessible to horses and mules). Only a few of these trails are described below, chosen as being particularly rewarding from the point of view of scenery and general interest. The distances and times apply to the outward and return journeys, unless otherwise specified.

YOSEMITE VALLEY

Mirror Lake Loop Trail   E

4.8 km (3 miles), 1½ hours

Begins and ends at Mirror Lake, accessible from Yosemite Village by an easy, flat path 1.6 km (1 mile) long. It runs in a circle starting with the lake on its left (splendid view of the Half Dome), climbs Tenaya Canyon (rocks smoothed by ice), crosses Tenaya Creek and then descends the other side of the valley to the point of departure. Easy walk.

Sentinel Dome Trail   E

4 km (2½ miles), 130 m (426 ft) change in elevation, 1½ hours

Begins at Glacier Point Road; ends at the top of the Sentinel Dome (2,746 m/9,007 ft). A short and easy

---

USEFUL ADVICE

It is absolutely essential to take great care over the packing and handling of any food that you are carrying. Bears are attracted by the smell and in their attempts to filch it, they cause thousands of dollars worth of damage to motor vehicles, camping equipment, and personal belongings every year. It is advisable, therefore, not to leave any food unattended either inside the car or in any form of containers outside. People who are careless about food are liable to heavy fines. Detailed information concerning the bears and precautions to take against them are in any event available at the park entrances and at the campgrounds.

Permits for expeditions of several days can be booked in advance from the Park's Backcountry Office.

Rivers, streams and waterfalls can always be dangerous, but especially when the water flow is heavy. Approach them carefully and take great care not to slip; strong currents and cold water can sometimes prove fatal. For the same reasons, it is advisable not to go bathing upstream of falls and near rapids.

CLIMATE

Yosemite enjoys a temperate climate, conducive to open-air activities all year round. Summer days are warm and dry: the temperature sometimes reaches 37°C (98°F) in the valleys and 24°C (75°F) at high altitude, but nights are always cool. Sometimes there can be storms during the afternoon.

In winter the temperature of the Yosemite Valley may drop to −15/12°C (4/10°F), although normally it hovers around −6°/+4°C (21/39°F), and may even climb to over 18°C (64°F). At the bottom of the valley the first snows fall in December, so much so that the Tioga Road may be closed for six to nine months a year.

PICNIC AREAS AND CAMPGROUNDS

There are picnic areas scattered throughout the park, along the roads and at viewpoints.

There are fourteen official campgrounds accessible by car: the five in the Yosemite Valley may be booked in advance (contact the Ticketron Reservations Offices), while the others are run on a system of "first come, first served." All accept both tents and trailers (charges vary from $5 to $10) and for limited periods (10/14 days according to season and locality). There are many other campgrounds outside the park, along the access highways.

Hikers can also make use of the High Sierra Camps, the five organized camps with tents in place, restaurant service and hot showers; these are open only in summer and advance booking is necessary. .

Free camping is controlled and in some parts of the park expressly forbidden. It is therefore advisable to get information beforehand when applying for permits for trips lasting several days.

walk which will take you to the summit of the granite Sentinel Dome, a marvellous viewpoint.

Inspiration Point Trail   M

4 km (2½ miles), 370 m (1,214 ft) change in elevation, 2 hours

Begins at the eastern end of the Wawona Tunnel; ends at Old Inspiration Point. This trail follows the path of the old Wawona Road, constructed in 1875 and used until the completion of the present road in 1933. It constitutes the final panoramic stretch of the Pohono Trail.

Vernal and Nevada Falls Trail   M

5.5 km (3½ miles), 600 m (1,968 ft) change in elevation, 3 hours

Begins at Happy Isles; ends at the top of the Nevada Fall. This "falls" route constitutes the initial stretch both of the Half Dome Trail and the John Muir Trail, which terminates on Mount Whitney, more than 340 km (212 miles) away.

Yosemite Falls Trail   M

11.5 km (7¼ miles), 820 m (2,690 ft) change in elevation, 5 hours

Begins at the Sunnyside campground; ends above the Yosemite Falls. This arduous trail takes you to the top of the second highest waterfall in the world (740 m/2,427 ft), from which there is a magnificent view of the Yosemite Valley. The falls are particularly impressive in spring when swollen by the thaw.

Four-Mile Trail   **M**

7.7 km (4¾ miles) outward only, 970 m (3,182 ft) change in elevation, 3 hours

Begins at the Four-Mile Trail car park, 2 km (1¼ miles) from Yosemite Village on Southside Drive; ends at Glacier Point. This panoramic trail, which follows the old road to Glacier Point, constructed in 1871, is fairly strenuous. The departure point is close to the base of Sentinel Rock, an impressive granite pinnacle 936 m (3,070 ft) high.

Panorama Trail   **M**

13.6 km (8½ miles), outward only, 975 m (3,198 ft) change in elevation, 4½ hours

Begins at Glacier Point (2,199 m/7,213 ft); ends at Happy Isles. This path is normally combined with Four-Mile Trail as a descent route, but can equally well be done in the opposite direction. The last 3 km (2 miles) or so coincide with the John Muir Trail.

Some of the most beautiful landscapes in California are to be found in the Sierra Nevada, the mountain range which runs parallel to the state's borders with Nevada for more than 400 km (250 miles). The principal tourist attraction of this mountain region is the Yosemite National Park, 4,800 km² (1,243 sq. miles) of peaks, valleys, granite monoliths, forests and waterfalls. In addition to its purely scenic attractions Yosemite offers a wide range of summer and winter recreational activities, including miles of trails to suit all tastes.

YOSEMITE VALLEY

Yosemite Valley, although covering an area of less than one per cent of the whole of Yosemite National Park, contains a cross-section of all the types of environment that can be found there. Many visitors tend to identify the valley with the park itself and although this imposes limitations, failing to do justice to the beauty of many other areas, it does give some idea of the spectacular nature of what has been described as the most beautiful valley in the world.

This region, however, is not merely scenic: the history of its elements are a great source of interest from an educational point of view; here, more than anywhere else, it is possible to understand the cataclysmic events that have moulded the mountains of the Sierra Nevada.

Between 250 and 80 million years ago, complex movements of the earth's crust affected the area nowadays occupied by California, creating several mountain ranges, including the Sierra Nevada. The rocks that made up the old Sierra, mostly metamorphic, were gradually and almost completely eroded, exposing huge slabs of hard granite (batholites) which formed after the cooling of the magma deep inside the earth's crust. These batholites make up the granite peaks which today characterize the landscape, not only of the Yosemite Valley but also of other parts of the Sierra Nevada, such as the Sequoia and Kings Canyon National Parks. Granite is a grey or pink rock (there are various types), with very compact, clearly visible crystals. By reason of its structural features, this is one of the finest areas for rock climbing; hence Yosemite boasts mountains which have become legendary, such as El Capitan, Half Dome (pictured below) and many others; it was on these walls, during the Seventies, that free-climbing – now recognized as an accredited sport all over the world – was first introduced.

These mountains have taken on their present appearance through the constant formative action of atmospheric factors, in addition to the continuation of crustal movements. Chiefly responsible is water, both in liquid and solid form. In particular, the action of the Quaternary glaci-

ations (30,000 years ago) left its clear imprint on the bare rock surfaces, which appear typically smooth and striated, and in the form both of valleys and mountains. Yosemite Valley is, from this point of view, a striking example of a valley of glacial origin, recognizable by its characteristic transversely U-shaped profile. Other visible signs are the numerous waterfalls, such as the Bridalveil Fall and the Yosemite Falls, which hurtle down from the hanging valleys, and the countless alpine lakes which nestle in the bowls of rock carved from the heads of long-vanished glaciers. However, the natural domes, which are perhaps the most famous features of the regional landscape, have a different origin. Half Dome, Sentinel Dome and El Capitan are all due to exfoliation; they were formed as a result of complex mechanical and physical phenomena associated with temperature and pressure. With the erosion of the rocks above, which were heaped up to a height of between 8 and 15 km (5 and 9½ miles), and the consequent decrease in pressure, some batholites began to expand (giving, as it

were, an enormous sigh of relief). This movement, in the case of the more compact and smooth varieties of granite, led to parallel ruptures on the surface, arranged in concentric lines, making the rock similar to an onion which gradually peeled off in scales or flakes – the process known as exfoliation.

Many trails offer visitors the chance to see lakes and waterfalls at close hand and to climb the peaks which dominate Yosemite Valley; some of them are long and arduous, such as the Half Dome Trail, whereas others are short, pleasant walks, like the Bridalveil Trail (only 30 minutes). For a comprehensive view of the whole valley, the best scenic position is Glacier Point, accessible also by car (but not in winter when the road is closed).

Because of the large number of tourists who throng the valley in the summer, the best time to visit it is out of season. You can help to reduce the overall pressure by not taking a car through the valley (there is an excellent bus service) and spending more time in other areas which are much less popular but equally beautiful.

Pohono Trail   M

21 km (13 miles), outward only, 550 m (1,804 ft) change in elevation in descent, 7 hours

Begins at Glacier Point; ends at the Wawona Tunnel, on the road of that name. This trail is normally followed in its descent: highly scenic, at three different points it looks down on the Yosemite Valley below. It is noted for its wealth of spring flowers.

Half Dome Trail   D

27 km (17 miles), 1,470 m (4,822 ft) change in elevation, 11 hours

Begins at Happy Isles; ends at the summit of the Half Dome (2,698 m/8,849 ft). The initial stretch coincides with the Vernal and Nevada Falls Trail; it then continues along the Little Yosemite Valley, rounds the Half Dome and ascends it on the opposite side to the great rock wall that dominates Yosemite Valley. The final 200 m (655 ft) are very steep and have fixed ropes for climbing. It is best to take two days over this trip and camp in the Little Yosemite Valley (permit needed).

TIOGA ROAD

A number of trails begin along this road, which crosses the park from west to east, and some of the easier ones are briefly described here; they come under the category of walks rather than genuine hikes.

North Dome Trail   M

6 km (3¾ miles) outward only

Begins 2 km (1¼ miles) after the Porcupine Flat campground; ends at the summit of the North Dome, the mountain that looks down on Yosemite Valley. A path links it with the Yosemite Falls Trail.

Lembert Dome Trail   E

3.8 km (2½ miles), 260 m (853 ft) change in elevation, 2 hours

Begins at Tuolumne Meadows; ends at the summit of Lembert Dome (2,880 m/9,447 ft). It is a branch off the Dog Lake Trail leading to the top of the charac-

teristic Lembert Dome, whose outline can be seen looming over the Tuolumne Meadows.

Elizabeth Lake Trail   E

9.6 km (6 miles), 4 hours

Begins at Tuolumne Meadows; ends at Elizabeth Lake. This is a gentle walk to a typical alpine lake, dominated by the mass of Unicorn Peak. A similar route, though slightly longer, follows a stretch of the John Muir Trail to Cathedral Lakes.

MORE DEMANDING TRAILS

Even the remotest corners of the Yosemite are accessible by trails, and it is possible to walk for months without passing the same spot. Two long, high trails wind for a certain distance through the park: the Pacific Crest trail and the John Muir Trail, which meet at Tuolumne Meadows. This area, second in importance to the Yosemite Valley, is not only a place of rare beauty but also a central point for trekking. Indeed, it marks the start of one of the park's most famous trails: the High Sierra Camps Loop Trail.

This is a circular route in six stages, which only requires a certain degree of fitness; because it presents no difficulties, it provides a marvellous opportunity even for the least experienced hikers.

Five camps, about 13 km (8 miles) apart from one another, serve as stopping points; these camps are furnished with beds (complete with sheets), toilets, hot showers and a large tent where meals are served.

They are open from early July to September inclusive, and advance booking is necessary. There is also an area attached to each camp reserved for those wishing to pitch their own tents.

High Sierra Camps Loop Trail

First stage: Toulumne Meadows-Glen Aulin Camp (12.2 km/7½ miles)
The trail begins at Tuolumne Meadows (2,621 m/ 8,597 ft), which can be reached by car or public transport. There are plenty of places to stay here. The route follows the Tuolumne River through broad alpine meadows and past a number of falls. Glen Aulin Camp lies at the foot of the White Cascade,

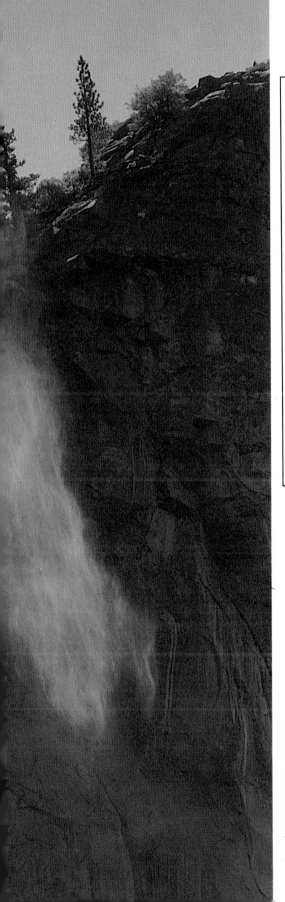

PHOTOGRAPHIC HINTS

Yosemite, like Sequoia and Kings Canyon, is a park of high mountains, where the green outlines of the forest make a striking contrast with the harsh greys of the granite walls. If you choose your lighting carefully, it is possible to take original and interesting shots. For excellent photographs of the lakes, which harbour amazing reflections when the water is calm, use a wide-angled lens, coupled with a good polarizing filter.

Because there are so many tall trees, it is worth avoiding dawn and dusk for grand overall views as they would be spoiled by broad areas of shadow. For the characteristic falls (especially the Bridalveil Fall, pictured on the left) you will need a 200 mm lens firmly fixed on a strong tripod. Then wait for a moment when the gusts of wind scatter the water spray over the widest possible area. The most spectacular shots can be obtained when the light comes from the side, illuminating only the waterfall and leaving the background in darkness.

On pages 100 and 101: the most famous of the several geological marvels of the Yosemite Valley is El Capitan, the biggest monolith in the world. A huge, steep outcrop, it has only a single fracture on its perpendicular wall. Its height is 2,308 m (7,570 ft) and it offers a real challenge even to expert free-climbers.

ANSEL ADAMS

The lakes of the Yosemite National Park were one of the favourite subjects of the famous American photographer Ansel Adams whose black and white pictures are among the finest masterpieces of the art. It was during a vacation in this region in 1916 that he was given his first camera, which he promptly used to record his impressions of the valley's beauty. These events were to have a great effect on his future because, in fact, he was to return every summer to Yosemite and photography was to become his lifetime career. The time he spent there and his expeditions inside the park nurtured his love for the mountains. As he wandered at will through this wild, empty region, he felt a sense of mystery and majesty so powerful that it seemed incumbent upon him to attempt to reproduce its wonders in his photographs. In his work, light played a fundamental role. Rather than rely simply on natural light falling directly on the object, he would achieve more revealing effects by taking his pictures, for example, in the early morning or late afternoon, or under a stormy sky. One of the lakes photographed by Ansel Adams was Tenaya Lake (shown on page 107), which is in the central-eastern part of the park.

on the shore of a lake where bathing is possible.
Second stage: Glen Aulin Camp-May Lake Camp (13.8 km/8½ miles)
Leaving Glen Aulin, you follow the McGee Lake Trail up past McGee Lake and across meadows rich in alpine flowers. The camp (2,825 m/9,266 ft) is situated on the eastern shore of May Lake, dominated by Mount Hoffmann (3,307 m/10,847 ft).
Third stage: May Lake Camp-Sunrise Camp (12.8 km/7 miles)
After a descent of about 300 m (984 ft), the trail crosses the Tioga Road Tenaya Lake and then ascends to the Forsyth Pass, beyond which are the three Sunrise Lakes. For Sunrise Camp (2,685 m/8,807 ft) you cross another pass and descend to Long Meadow.
Fourth stage: Sunrise Camp-Merced Lake Camp (13 km/8¼ miles)
The trail descends, following the course of Echo Creek and Merced River. The camp is at the eastern end of Merced Lake, tucked away in a forest of tall conifers at an altitude of only 2,217 m (7,272 ft).
Fifth stage: Merced Lake Camp-Vogelsang Camp (14.5 or 12.2 km/9 or 7½ miles)
There are two possible routes from Merced Lake Camp. One trail climbs the valley of Lewis Creek to the Vogelsang Pass (3,261 m/10,696 ft), from which there is a descent to Vogelsang Camp (3,096 m/10,155 ft). This is the longer and more strenuous route, but also the more scenic. The alternative is to follow Fletcher Creek from Merced Lake; the trail ascends gradually through high meadows. Vogelsang Camp is the highest of the five encountered along the entire trail.
Sixth stage: Vogelsang Camp-Toulumne Meadows (11.6 or 19.8 km/7¼ or 12½ miles)
For this last stage there are also two possible routes. The shorter option, when leaving Vogelsang Camp, is to cross the Tuolumne Pass and descend along Rafferty Creek until you join the John Muir Trail which leads to Tuolumne. Alternatively, you leave the camp and follow first Ireland Creek Trail and, where this ends, join the John Muir Trail.

FAUNA

The most conspicuous animal in the park, the mule deer (*Odocoileus hemionus*), known for its long mule-like ears and black-tipped tail, ranges widely over the chaparral, through the conifer forests, alpine meadows and many other habitats. It is the only ungulate living in the park and although it is not shy and is easy to approach, it is nonetheless a wild animal and should not be touched or fed. The same precautions apply to the black bear (*Ursus americanus*) which, in spite of its name, may be variable in colour from pale yellow, to brown and black. This bear, though widely distributed in much of the United States, is particularly common in Yosemite, which is undoubtedly the protected area where it can be most easily observed.

Sometimes it is also possible to catch sight of the coyote, the raccoon, the grey fox and the porcupine; rarer still are sightings of the bay lynx or the puma. On the other hand, squirrels can be spotted everywhere: the grey squirrel is active practically all year round. There are five species of chipmunk, in addition to the small and noisy Douglas squirrel, which inhabits the conifer forests. Alpine animals include the yellow-bellied marmot (*Marmota flaviventris*), pictured below, the biggest rodent in the park, and the pika (*Ochotona princeps*), a small mammal similar to a tailless rabbit which lives in the stony areas at the upper limit of the tree line.

Birds are represented by more than 200 species. Very common in Yosemite Valley are Steller's jay (*Cyanocitta stelleri*), with its typical tuft, various types of woodpecker and the western meadowlark (*Sturnella neglecta*). Higher up, the bird population changes; among the many birds which nest in the mountains are a few which are conspicuous for their brilliant plumage, such as the mountain bluebird (*Sialia currucoides*), or for their noisy chatter, like Clark's nutcracker (*Nucifraga columbiana*) and the little mountain chickadee (*Parus gambeli*).

FLORA

Between the altitudes of 600 m (1,968 ft) on the western boundaries and 3,900 m (12,792 ft) at the eastern peaks, there are innumerable habitats which harbour a wide range of plant growth. In the park thirty-seven tree species, both broadleaved and coniferous, grow wild, in addition to 1,400 different flower species. As always, the vegetation is structured in bands or belts, overlapping here and there, and determined principally by altitude. The road access to the park from the west crosses a hilly zone of between about 600 m (1,968 ft) and 900 m (2,952 ft), which is notable for the chaparral, a community of shrubby plants in dense thickets which are adapted to the hotter, drier climate of the lowlands, mixed with thin woods of pine and oak. In spring the chaparral is bright with the colours of dozens of flower species, including the golden orange California poppy (*Eschscholzia californica*). Between 900 m (2,952 ft) and about 2,000 m (6,560 ft) there is a broad expanse of conifers (photographs below and on right), with one or two species dominating the areas depending on the type of soil and amount of rainfall. They include the western yellow pine (*Pinus ponderosa*), the Jeffrey pine (*P. jeffreyi*), the sugar pine (*P. lambertiana*), the incense cedar (*Calocedrus decurrens*), which is often mistaken for a sequoia, and the Douglas fir or Douglas spruce (*Pseudotsuga menziesii*).

Another tree that grows in this belt, which includes the Yosemite Valley, is the California black oak (*Quercus kelloggii*), common on dry soil. There are also the only three groves of giant sequoias in the park here: Mariposa Grove, Tuolumne Grove and Merced Grove. Above a height of 2,000 m (6,560 ft) the smaller conifers give way to the California red fir (*Abies magnifica*) and the lodgepole or twisted pine (*P. contorta*); the former tends to form almost entire forests, but where the soil is too thin it is the latter that is more successful. Among the very considerable number of mountain flowers which grow at these altitudes, along the trails and in the meadows, is the rare Washington lily (*Lilium washingtonianum*), recognizable by its large white flowers borne on a very tall stalk, 1.8 m (6 ft) high. Above 2,800 m (9,184 ft), the forests thin out progressively to the point where only a few isolated trees manage to grow: the mountain hemlock (*Tsuga mertensia*), the western white pine (*P. monticola*) and the whitebarked pine (*P. albicaulis*), which in the Sierra Nevada itself flourishes at over 3,000 m (9,840 ft). Here, the cold and the wind cause it to adopt twisted forms, like a natural bonsai which will take up to 200 years before producing seeds. In these extremely harsh surroundings, many alpine plants are still able to find favourable conditions to grow in, including the cross-leaved heath (*Erica tetralix*), with its small campanulate flowers.

DEVILS POSTPILE NATIONAL MONUMENT

Access: From US 395 following State 203 to Minaret Summit (16 km/10 miles), then 11 km (7 miles) of dirt road.

Points of interest: Devils Postpile, situated at an altitude of 2,500 m (8,200 ft) on the western side of the Sierra Nevada in a region of lakes and forests, southeast of the Yosemite National Park, is a marvellous example of columnar fissuring in a basaltic outflow (photograph below). This unique phenomenon appears at the surface of a cooled lava mass and is due to the contraction which follows the actual cooling process. The columns are formed when the basaltic outflows begin to erode, breaking up the rock into huge prisms, polygonal in cross-section (and often so regular as to be hexagonal), their length being perpendicular to the outer surface of cooling. The columns of the Devils Postpile stand 12–18 m (40–60 ft) high and originated some 100,000 years ago. The Monument is managed by the Ranger Station, which serves as a visitor center, picnic area and campground ($5 a night's stay, no advance booking, open 20 June to 1 October, according to weather). There are no shops or service stations here.

The area is crossed from north to south by the John Muir Trail and towards the west by the King Creek Trail; there are also shorter trails. Free camping is not permitted, nor are off-trail exped-

itions. The Monument is open from end June to October. For information contact the Park Manager, Devils Postpile National Monument, PO Box 50, Mammoth Lake, California 93546, tel. (619) 934-2289 (summer and autumn) or (209) 565-3341 (winter and spring).

Photographic hints: The Devils Postpile columns are excellent subjects, either in a group or in interesting close-up compositions. The outlines of these giant organ pipes, all perfectly parallel and visibly radial, can make a fascinating and challenging subject. It is worth waiting until the sunlight (in summer early in the afternoon) strikes the columns from above, so that the shadows heighten the effect of shapes and volumes. It is best to use a 200 mm or 300 mm telephoto lens.

LAKE TAHOE

Access: Although more than 200 km (125 miles) away, the lake is easily accessible by the Tioga Road and then US 395. In summer it is linked with Yosemite by a public bus service.

Points of interest: The lake (photograph below), situated on the borders of California and Nevada, lies at the foot of the eastern slopes of the Sierra Nevada; it is a region full of lakes and forests which is ideal for long treks. The surroundings are in every way like those of Yosemite, Kings Canyon and Sequoia, although rather more built up, but the lake itself, with the various facilities for tourists, offers a larger range of recreational activities, especially water sports.

FLORIDA

EVERGLADES
NATIONAL PARK

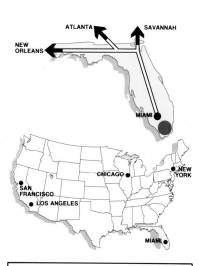

The southernmost tip of Florida, a peninsula point-
ing towards the Caribbean, is a boundless area of
swampland which gradually tapers into the sea. It is
actually a river, and perhaps the oddest in the world,
flowing slowly from Lake Okeechobee in a south-
westerly direction into the Gulf of Mexico. Originally, before man modified it, the river measured 64
–112 km (40–70 miles) across, 160 km (100 miles) in
length and 15 cm (6 in) in depth, inclining on average
4 cm/km and flowing at a speed of 800 m (2,624 ft) a
day.

The river's appearance is still that which led the
Indians to call it "Pa-hay-okee" which means "river
of grass," although today it is known the world over
as Everglades. The National Park of that name protects only a part of it, some 5,700 km² (2,200 sq.
miles) of swamps, mangrove forests, pinewoods and
cypress groves, "islands" of tropical jungle,
estuaries, islets and a broad arm of sea off the tip of
the peninsula. This huge variety of habitats
accommodates a very rich and unique flora and
fauna. However, of all the protected areas in the
United States, the Everglades National Park is the
most seriously threatened by human pressure and it
has the longest list of endangered animals.

Address: Superintendent, Everglades
National Park, PO Box 279, Home-
stead, Florida 33030, tel. (305) 247-6211.
Area: 5,700 km² (2,200 sq. miles).
Altitude: At sea level.
Access: Main entrance on State High-
way 9336, 20 km (12½ miles) southwest
of Homestead. A second entrance at
Shark Valley on Interstate 41.
Opening times: Main entrance is open
all year round, 24 hours a day. Shark
Valley from 8.30 am to 6 pm.
Entry charge: At the main entrance $5
per car or $2 per person on foot, by
bicycle or on public transport; at Shark
Valley the respective charges are $3 and
$1, valid for 7 days. Golden Eagle Pass-
port valid.

The Indians of yesterday and today

Enormous heaps of shell fragments, easily mistaken
at first glance for small hills, constitute the earliest
evidence of human presence in the Everglades region, dating back at least 11,000 years. In the most
westerly section of the park, Gulf Coast, several of

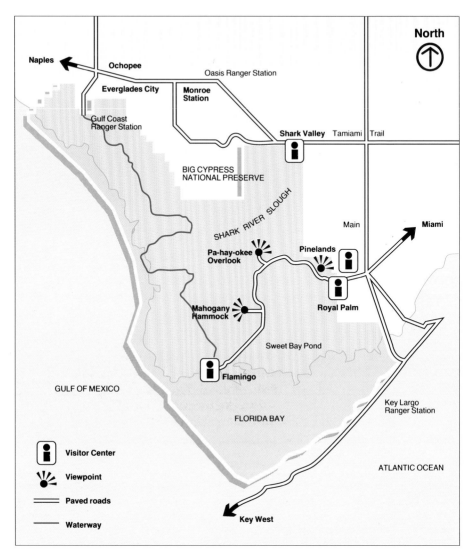

North

Naples

Ochopee

Oasis Ranger Station

Everglades City

Monroe Station

Gulf Coast Ranger Station

Shark Valley Tamiami Trail

BIG CYPRESS NATIONAL PRESERVE

SHARK RIVER SLOUGH

Main

Miami

Pa-hay-okee Overlook

Pinelands

Mahogany Hammock

Royal Palm

Sweet Bay Pond

Flamingo

GULF OF MEXICO

Key Largo Ranger Station

FLORIDA BAY

ATLANTIC OCEAN

Visitor Center

Viewpoint

Paved roads

Waterway

Key West

Fuel: The park's only service station is at Flamingo; outside they are at Homestead, Everglades City and on the Tamiami Trail near Shark Valley.

Roads: One paved road, 61 km (38 miles) long, crosses the park from the main entrance to Flamingo, the most southerly tourist station. The road from Shark Valley is closed to traffic and off-trail driving is forbidden throughout the park.

Shops: At Flamingo.

Accommodation: Motel and cabins at Flamingo (from 1 May to 31 October many facilities are closed); for information and advance booking apply to Flamingo Lodge, PO Box 428, Flamingo, Florida 33030, tel. (813) 695-3101 or (305) 253-2241.

Visitor Center: There are five: at the main entrance, Royal Palm, Flamingo, Shark Valley and Everglades City. They provide information, land maps and nautical charts, publications, permanent exhibitions and audio-visual material. Open from 8 am to 5 pm.

Guided tours: The park's naturalists organize expeditions all year round, trips in boats and canoes, and evening conferences. Programmes are displayed at the Visitor Centers.

Other activities: Expeditions of varying lengths in canoes and motorboats (which can be hired at Flamingo and in Everglades City), cycling, birdwatching and fishing (license necessary).

Beware of: Insect bites (mosquitoes) and violent summer storms.

the largest mounds, up to 6 m (20 ft) high, are to be found, and their origin is still uncertain. Probably at one time the mounds were simply piles of discarded shells, and only later were they used for burials and religious rites, as well as providing shelter against the violent ocean storms which battered the coastal settlements. The natives responsible for building them were permanently settled in this zone where they could find an abundance of food: oysters and other molluscs, crustaceans, fish, turtles, birds, small mammals, deer and even manatees were easy prey, and these, supplemented by seeds and other plants, made up a varied and balanced diet.

When Florida was occupied by the Spaniards, at the beginning of the sixteenth century, the Indians who inhabited the Everglades must have numbered several thousand. These were divided into two groups. The more numerous lived on the Gulf Coast and were made up of the Calusa, while along the southern and southeastern coasts of the peninsula were the Tequesta. Needless to say, within only three centuries both tribes had been decimated by diseases introduced by the invaders (from the common cold to tuberculosis) and reduced to a scattered group of survivors.

Their place was taken, in due course, by other Indians from Carolina, Alabama and Georgia: the Miccosukee and the Muskogee, collectively known as Seminoles. Expelled from their original homes first by the English and then the American colonists, these Indians were not left in peace even when settled in the Everglades. The hospitality they extended to fugitive negro slaves and the raids carried out on nearby farms were sufficient pretext for their being wiped out once and for all, and deported en masse to a reserve. This operation cost the lives of hundreds of soldiers, as well as millions of dollars, and ended with the segregation of Chief Billy Bowlegs and another 164 Seminoles inside the reserve. A certain number of Miccosukee managed nevertheless to hide in the heart of the Everglades and to preserve their culture to the present day, often thanks only to the changes effected by time and by man.

The park and the tomatoes

In 1905 the assassination of the hunting officer deputed by the Audubon Society to safeguard the birds

USEFUL ADVICE

In the Everglades virtually any type of activity, particularly walking, is best done in winter, both because the climate is more suitable and because there is no longer such a big problem with mosquitoes. However, Christmas is a time when the park is especially crowded, so if you want to avoid difficulties in finding accommodation in the campgrounds or at Flamingo Lodge, it is best to choose another period.

The mosquito problem should not be underestimated, even in winter, but a few simple precautions can help to avoid the pain and discomfort. The most obvious is to use insect repellants, which can always be bought in the park if you do not have any; secondly, and especially if you are making long expeditions on foot, make sure to wear long-sleeved sweaters, long trousers and some form of head covering; thirdly, if you intend to camp, use only tents furnished with mosquito nets.

There is no danger from animals, although it is wise to keep well clear of crocodiles and alligators and on no account try to feed them; these reptiles may appear slow and clumsy but in fact they are capable of making sudden violent moves. The venomous snakes are shy by nature and will not normally constitute a problem if left undisturbed.

CLIMATE

The climate of the park is decidedly subtropical; only two seasons, dry and rainy, alternate with virtually nothing in between. During winter, from November to April, weather conditions are almost always perfect, with little rain and mild temperatures; the temperature seldom falls below zero centigrade.

On the other hand, in the summer months, from May to October, 80 per cent of the precipitation occurs, the average annual incidence of rainfall being 127 cm (50 in), swelling the water level of the Everglades lakes, swamps and canals. The rain is carried by gigantic cumulo-nimbus clouds which cause extremely violent storms that may last a few minutes and be repeated several times a day. Moreover, in summer the daytime temperatures are almost always over 32°C (89°F). The mosquitoes, which thrive in a hot, humid climate, make it virtually impossible to spend much time in the park at this time.

from poachers, at a time when there was a thriving trade in feathers for adorning ladies' hats, marked the serious launch of campaigns for the protection of the Everglades. For some time naturalists and conservationists had demanded an end to the havoc which was devastating southern Florida, with farmers, timber merchants and poachers outvying one another in the destruction of plants and animals. Even so, despite the efforts of many people and associations, often economically substantial, the National Park was not inaugurated until 6 December 1947 – further evidence that the financial lobbies of the east coast wielded far more power than their counterparts on the west coast.

The foundation of the park, however, has not been sufficient to avert the most serious danger, that of "dying of thirst." Water, which literally brings life to the vast swamps and complex network of habitats within them, is no longer allowed to flow freely. Massive hydraulic works (dams, locks, canals and aqueducts, etc.) were carried out not only upriver of the park, where the catchment basin feeding the "river of grass" originated, but also right outside its boundaries. The water taken from the Everglades is used to slake the thirst of 3.5 million people and to irrigate the rocky ground of Dade County where, among other crops, 75 per cent of the United States'

winter tomatoes are grown!

Everglades has thus had to face the same problems as those afflicting Mono Lake in California: it is not a question of neglecting the needs of humans but simply of avoiding waste, to ensure that an environment of world importance, established as an international reserve for the benefit of mankind, does not vanish from the earth.

Marked trails

Walking in the Everglades, where earth and water meet, is a unique experience. The trails, in fact, are never completely dry, except for those made of raised walkways, and the hiker often has to negotiate stretches where the water comes up to the ankles or even to the knees. It also involves a different kind of physical test: instead of ascents and descents, there is a hot, humid climate.

The consequence is that in this region, where it is hard to trace a clear dividing line between land and water, it is not easy to distinguish those trails which can be attempted on foot from those that must be negotiated by canoe. On the other hand, the most fascinating and exciting trails are actually the areas which combine the two forms of transport.

Inside the park, however, in keeping with the best

Fed by the waters of the enormous Lake Okeechobee, in southern Florida, the Everglades give some idea of what the whole of the more southerly part of the state must once have looked like; a boundless expanse of marshes, mangrove swamps, carnivorous plants, woods and trees, with millions of birds, fish, snakes and alligators, not to mention insects, particularly mosquitoes. This swamp is actually a freshwater river (its Indian name is Pa-Hay-Okee, meaning "river of grass"), on average 80 km (50 miles) wide, 160 km (100 miles) long and only a few centimeters deep. This strange river has an incline of a mere 2 cm per kilometer and flows so slowly that a single drop of water from the lake would take years to reach the gulf.

PICNIC AREAS AND CAMPGROUNDS

In the park there are only four proper picnic grounds with tables, cooking areas and toilet facilities – at Long Pine Key, along the Flamingo Road and at Flamingo.

There are two campgrounds: the one at Long Pine Key is 8 km (5 miles) from the main entrance and has 108 places for tents or trailers, with toilets but no showers; the one at Flamingo has 300 places, 60 of which are reserved for those without cars (walk-in sites), with toilets and showers (no hot water). Charges are $7 per night for the normal tent sites and $4 for the walk-in sites at Flamingo. In both campgrounds tent sites reserved for organized groups (from 6 to 15 persons) cost $10 per night and an advance booking should be made in writing not more than 90 days beforehand to Group Camping Reservations. No booking is accepted for other places and the time limit of any stay is 14 days from December to 31 March or a total of 30 days in a year. In January, February and March both campgrounds are generally overcrowded, so it is advisable to arrive early in the morning to reserve your spot. There is a general store near the Flamingo campground, while those intending to camp at Long Pine Key should buy all they need at Homestead.

There are 32 allotted areas for free camping, consisting mainly of wooden platforms raised above ground level. Most of these are only accessible by boat or canoe. A Backcountry Permit can be obtained from the Visitor Centers and Ranger Stations which provide all the necessary information about camping regulations.

Paradise Key where ferns, exotic plants and small trees grow.

On pages 118 and 119: a group of ardeids in a pond near Everglades City.

national traditions in management of protected areas, there are numerous marked trails which, sparing visitors difficulties and inconveniences, enable them to appreciate the different natural habitats and to observe the most typical plants and animals. Most of these trails, described below, are "interpretative," that is to say accompanied by informative panels or described in small guides which draw attention to their natural features. The distances apply to the outward and return journeys, unless otherwise specified. Given the shortness of the trails, no times have been included. Those marked with an asterisk are also accessible to people in wheelchairs.

Pa-hay-okee Overlook Trail   E

0.4 km (¼ mile)

This trail branches off the Flamingo Road, about 20 km (12½ miles) from the main park entrance, and leads to a raised viewpoint. From this platform there is a comprehensive view of the Shark River Slough, the Miccosukees' "river of grass," punctuated by hammocks, the pieces of elevated land in the swamps.

Anhinga Trail*   E

0.5 km (⅓ mile)

Begins and ends at the Royal Palm Visitor Center. A circular trail, partly on wooden walkways and partly on a paved path, which offers one of the best opportunities of seeing at close-hand alligators, snakes, turtles and numerous birds, including herons, egrets and anhingas or snakebirds (*Anhinga anhinga*), after which the trail is named. These splendid birds, which feed on fish swallowed whole, nest in colonies close to the trail towards the end of winter.

Gumbo-Limbo Trail   E

0.5 km (⅓ mile)

Begins and ends at the Royal Palm Visitor Center. This trail runs through a typical hammock, these islets of dense tropical vegetation where the gumbo-limbo (*Roystonea elata*), recognizable by its thin reddish-brown bark, grows along with an infinite variety of epiphytes (orchids, bromeliads, ferns, etc.).

Mahogany Hammock Trail* E

0.5 km (⅓ mile)

Begins at the start of a short paved road which branches off halfway from the Flamingo Road. The trail, entirely on raised walkways, leads through a hammock notable for the growth of a small palm (*Acoelorrhaphe wrightii*), endemic to the Everglades, and the largest mahoganies in the United States. At night you can hear the cry of the barred owl (*Strix varia*).

Pinelands Trail E

0.8 km (½ mile)

A circular trail near the Flamingo Road, about 8 km (5 miles) from the main park entrance, and of considerable botanic interest.

The trail runs through a dry area occupied by a forest of *Pinus elliottii*, an environment determined by periodic fires, which harbours some 200 plant species, including thirty or so endemic ones. Along some stretches there are visible limestone outcrops of the Miami Formation which constitutes the rocky substratum of the Everglades.

Mangrove Wilderness Trail* E

0.8 km (½ mile)

The trail, entirely over walkways, leads through a mangrove forest which encircles the banks of West Lake, about 13 km (8 miles) before Flamingo. It is a typical brackish water environment, the habitat of numerous fish and crustaceans which find food and shelter among the mangrove roots.

Eco Pond Trail E

0.8 km (½ mile)

Circular trail around a freshwater pond near the Flamingo campground, ideal for birdwatching.

Bobcat Boardwalk and Otter Cave Trail E

These two short trails begin at the Shark Valley car park. Both offer good opportunities to glimpse the very rare Everglades kite.

THE STRANGLER FIG

The strangler fig or golden fig (*Ficus aurea*), is a typical Florida tree, the main characteristic of which is the presence of aerial roots which grasp and often strangle the tree which serves as its host (photograph opposite). Both the aerial roots and the branches which reach the ground can generate an independent root system. This evergreen with elliptical leaves produces small flowers which are yellow in bud and which later turn red. The fruits consist of small drupes contained in a fleshy outer layer which is yellow with reddish tints. The bark of the strangler fig is smooth and ash-grey in young specimens, becoming scaly in those with a broad trunk. It can grow to a height of 12–15 m (40–50 ft), with a diameter of 90 cm (3 ft).

*On pages 120 and 121: the silver trunks of cypress trees stand out against a blue winter sky. The areas richest in this tree (*Taxodium distichum) *are around Rock Reef Pass and Sweet Bay Pond.*

N.B. Many ponds, like Sisal Pond, Ficus Pond, Mrazek Pond and others along the Flamingo Road, are excellent places for viewing water birds and can be reached easily by the signposted paths.

MORE DEMANDING TRAILS

When embarking on the following trails, it is always advisable to carry a good supply of drinking water as there is none along the routes.

Snake Bight Trail   M

6.5 km (4 miles), 2 hours

Begins at Flamingo Road, 9.6 km (6 miles) before the Ranger Station; ends at the seashore. The well-marked trail follows the right bank of Snake Bight Channel through a tunnel of tropical vegetation. At the end of the trail is a raised walkway over the waters of Florida Bay. Return to the point of departure by the same route. Excellent for birdwatching.

Christian Point Trail   M

6.5 km (4 miles), 2 hours

Begins at Flamingo Road, 2.3 km (1½ miles) before the Ranger Station; ends at the seashore. The trail, signposted in white, crosses mangrove forests and coastal meadows alternately, terminating on the muddy southern banks of Snake Bight. Return to point of departure by the same route.

Bear Lake Trail   M

6.5 km (4 miles), 2 hours

Begins at the start of Bear Lake Road, a paved road of some 3 km (1¾ miles) which branches off the main road just before Flamingo. The trail skirts a canal, along which are many heaps of shell fragments put there by the Calusa and now covered in vegetation. In winter numerous American spoonbills can be observed on the lake. Return to the point of departure by the same route.

Rowdy Bend Trail   M

8 km (5 miles), 2½ hours

Begins at Flamingo Road, 5.3 km (3¼ miles) before

PHOTOGRAPHIC HINTS

The Everglades, like any vast expanse of ground uninterrupted by hills or mountains, provides few opportunities for pictures that give an overall idea of the landscape. The only possibility is to go up in a small tourists' aircraft, which can be hired quite cheaply in Everglades City or in Naples. But it is not necessary to resort to these lengths as there are more opportunities for taking interesting photographs than might at first appear, bearing in mind the wide variety of habitats offered by the park: the domes formed by the swamp cypresses, the intricacies of the mangrove swamps, the regular pattern of leaves of the saw palmetto (*Serenoa repens*), the roots of the strangler fig (pictured below), or the masses of ferns.

Given the dimensions of the horizon, it is better to only use a 35 mm lens for overall views; views with a lens any wider tend to make the line of the horizon far too distant, with a consequent loss of any interesting detail. A macro lens, on the other hand, is indispensable for taking pictures of the many flowers (especially the orchids), insects and other small animals in the area. In the case of bigger creatures a 400 mm telephoto lens is more suitable given the amount of distance which has to be kept from these animals if they are not to be frightened away.

Inside the forests it is best to work with even weaker light or an overcast sky, because sunlight, coming through the tangle of leaves and trunks, will create too much contrast between brightly illuminated and deeply shaded zones, which is hard to eliminate totally by compensation. Obviously, it is necessary in these circumstances to make use of a tripod. Also, a slightly amber-yellow filter will reduce the bluish tone that all films show in the absence of sun or in shadow.

A focal length of about 200 mm is invaluable for taking shots of the root structure of mangroves, veritable examples of natural architecture, or to highlight plants or trunks within a group of specimens of the same species.

Finally, a special word about alligators; excellent close-ups can be obtained in pictures of groups by shooting from a low level through a wide-angle lens.

FLORA

The Everglades are an enormous stretch of swamps and marshes – in other words, a vast wet zone, the ecology of which is determined by the presence, in varying amounts, of water. This may be fresh, salty or brackish, depending on the distance from the coast, and together with the irregularity of the terrain gives the plant cover a characteristic mosaic pattern. In fact the diverse types of vegetation, which are easily recognizable, visibly betray the different environmental conditions, such as salinity and the quantity of water in the soil. On the other hand, the lithological factor, that is the kind of rock underneath the vegetation, bears no weight in determining these variations given that in the Everglades it consists exclusively of limestone of the Miami Formation.

The immense stretches of wetland, covered in grass, are dominated by common sawgrass (*Mariscus jamaicensis*), a member of the sedge family (*Cyperaceae*) bearing long, narrow leaves with finely toothed margins that have given it its vernacular name; a walk through dense clumps of this grass can be a painful experience. Capable of withstanding winter drought as well as prolonged immersion of the roots in the wet season, the sawgrass originally covered an area of some 12,000 km^2 (4,635 sq. miles), literally a "sea" of grass. From what remains of this "sea," small islands of trees protrude here and there, according to the reliefs and depressions of the rocky limestone substratum. The depressions may be natural "bowls" or rather channels in which water flows slowly; in the former case the accumulation of sandy peat creates ideal conditions for the growth of the swamp cypress (*Taxodium distichum*), while in the latter instance there are "island" formations of the willow *Salix caroliniana*, a sturdy, adventurous species (pictured opposite), or thickets of *Chrysobalanus icaco*, *Persea borbonia*, *Magnolia virginiana*, *Ilex cassine* and *Rhus radicans*, where the water is shallower.

A tropical type of vegetation, formed of trees with roots which need to stay out of water, grows on rocky mounds 30–90 cm (1–3 ft) high. This community of so-called "hammocks" is made up in the main of palms and broadleaved species that are Asiatic in origin, such as the strangler fig (*Ficus aurea*), the mahogany (*Swietenia mahog-*

ani) and the gumbo-limbo (*Bursera simaruba*), mingled with trees from temperate regions, the commonest of which is the majestic oak *Quercus virginiana*. The branches and trunks of the hammock trees constitute an ideal habitat for countless epiphytic plants (photograph below); they are for the most part orchids, bromeliads and ferns which grow in the air, supporting themselves on large trees without doing them any harm. In fact they are merely guests and not parasites, similar to lichens, which in the shape of coloured crusts or long "beards" grow abundantly on bark. Where fire, a natural feature of vital importance to the ecology of the Everglades, repeatedly burns the limestone ridges, the hammock vegetation is replaced by pinewoods of *Pinus elliottii*, which contribute notably to the enrichment of the park's vegetation, harbouring some thirty species which are not found in any other association.

Finally, the broad coastal belt, where fresh water mingles with that of the ocean, is dominated by mangrove forests which cover about 26 per cent of the park's surface. Of the different species collectively known as "mangroves" the most typical is the red mangrove (*Rhizophora mangle*), recognizable at first glance by the long, curving roots which are immersed in the water. These trees, which according to species activate various mechanisms to withstand the water salinity, manage to colonize the smallest strips of land that emerge from the sea, thus helping to create countless islets that are the outposts of dry land proper.

the Ranger Station; ends at the crossing with the Snake Bight Trail. The path follows an old driveway through mangrove forests and coastal meadows. Combined with the Snake Bight Trail and a stretch of the Flamingo Road, it makes an interesting circular walk of about 11 km (7 miles) in all.

Coastal Prairie Trail   M

9.7 km (6 miles) outward only, 3 hours

Begins in front of the C-54 parking area of the Flamingo campground; ends at Clubhouse Beach. The trail follows an old road through wet, brackish zones and forests of *Conocarpus erectus*, a plant similar to the mangrove. The walk is ideal for examining the plant communities of the coastal belt.

At the end of the trail, well signposted throughout, is an area for free camping; camping permits are obtainable from the Flamingo Ranger Station. Return to the point of departure by the same route.

Long Pine Key Nature Trail   M

11.3 km (7 miles) outward only, 3½ hours

Begins at the Long Pine Key campground; ends on Flamingo Road. A network of well maintained forest paths, suitable also for bicycles, takes you through the characteristic pinewoods. This is the habitat of the rare Florida puma, an animal threatened with extinction.

Alligator Creek   M

11.8 km (7½ miles) outward only, 3½ hours

Begins at Snake Bight Canal Road, which branches off the park's main road, 9.6 km (6 miles) before Flamingo; ends at Alligator Creek. The first stretch coincides with the Snake Bight Canal Road (where cars can be parked) and then leaves it by branching off to the left on an old road leading through mangrove forests and coastal meadows to Alligator Creek.

There is a small area reserved for free camping.

Along the Tamiami Trail in Shark Valley visitors can admire an immense forest of mahogany trees which provides a home for many species of marshland birds.

FAUNA

The wide range of habitats to be found in the Everglades, highlighted by the numerous types of plants, supports an abundance of animal life. A myriad of species is represented, from land forms, such as the bay lynx or desert cat (*Lynx rufus*), pictured opposite, to arboreal, marine, and freshwater forms, as well as those adapted to transitional surroundings.

The warm, shallow waters of Florida Bay, a tract of sea that stretches for about 2,000 km^2 (773 sq. miles) south of the peninsula tip, are dotted with hundreds of little islands called "keys" (derived from the Spanish *cayos*, meaning "islet") covered in mangroves, which accommodate a large marine fauna, including molluscs, crustaceans and some fifty species of fish, plus two characteristic animals of these surroundings, the manatee (*Trichecus manatus*) and the green turtle (*Chelonia mydas mydas*). Both of these are herbivores, feeding on the algae and plants that make up the extensive submarine prairies, and both figure high on the list of endangered species. Others also found on this list are the Florida puma, the Everglades mink (*Mustela vison* spp.), the crocodile and numerous birds.

It is the range and variety of birdlife, more than anything else, which has made the Everglades famous all over the world. At least 326 different species have been counted in the park, of which 240 are regarded as sedentary or regular visitors. The best season for birdwatching and for photography is winter, when drought compels the birds, like all other animals, to gather around ponds and lakes. They fly off when summer storms raise the water level everywhere and enable them to scatter throughout the park. Among the most conspicuous and easily identifiable birds, both in coloration and size, are the American spoonbill (*Ajaja ajaja*), pictured below, pink with its distinctive bill, the great white heron (*Egretta alba*), with a long yellow bill and black legs, and other species that are superficially alike but whose shape of bill indicates the kind of diet and the method used for catching prey (plants and water invertebrates, frogs, fish, etc.).

More rare is the wood ibis (*Mycteria americana*), with a grey, featherless head, which nests in colonies on cypresses and goes hunting for fish in the surrounding ponds and lakes. This bird is seriously endangered by water extraction which, by altering the water cycle and lowering its level even around the interior of the park, reduces the amount of available food: the Everglades kite (*Rostrhamus sociabilis*), whose diet consists almost exclusively of small snails, only to be found in Shark Valley, is similarly threatened.

CROCODILES AND ALLIGATORS

The alligator (*Alligator mississippiensis*) is in a sense a symbol of the Everglades (photograph below), and really more for its appeal to artists and film-makers than for its zoological interest. It would be hard to deny that the majority of people visiting the park secretly hope they will have an exciting encounter with one, which actually is far from a realistic expectation. In fact, this huge reptile, which grows to 5 m (16½ ft) in length, has a calm disposition, happy to spend hours on end floating in a few inches of water. Such behaviour is basically physiological: being a cold-blooded creature, it has a fairly low metabolism, which enables it on the one hand to survive up to six months without eating (though normally it feeds once or twice a week), and on the other spares it no energy to be wasted uselessly. Turtles, water birds and waders, raccoons, small dogs and, occasionally, white-tailed deer fall prey to the alligator's powerful jaws, and, should their dimensions permit, they are swallowed whole.

Man does not figure in this list and, as further proof of the animal's lack of aggression, there are no recorded instances either of fatal incidents or of serious injury. Even so, it is absolutely forbidden to give food to the alligators because, apart from considerations of good wildlife management, there is no need to tempt them to the point of regarding a human arm as a potential morsel. But if the alligator, common in the lakes and ponds of the park (it has been successfully protected and is increasing in numbers), represents no danger to hikers, and the American crocodile (*Crocodylus acutus*) is even less of a threat. This reptile, of which there are no more than 300 specimens in the park, frequents brackish and saltwater habitats, principally Florida Bay where in fact a vast area has been closed to the public and is destined as a reserve wholly for the crocodiles.

The different habitat is not the only thing that distinguishes an alligator from a crocodile. As a rule identification is based on the form of the head, that of the alligator being U-shaped and that of the crocodile V-shaped; also the body colour of the alligator is mainly black and that of the crocodile grey-green. Moreover the crocodile is smaller, measuring not more than about 4 m (13 ft) long.

At this point you can either return by the same route to the Snake Bight Canal Road or continue by canoe along the West Lake Canoe Trail.

Old Ingraham Highway   M

21 km (13 miles) outward only, 7 hours

Begins at the Royal Palm Visitor Center; ends on Flamingo Road, about 3 km (1¾ miles) south of the diversion for Mahogany Hammock. This trail follows the old road to Flamingo, built before the inauguration of the park and abandoned in the 1940s (today it is closed to traffic). For a long stretch it runs along the Homestead Canal which in winter attracts many birds and alligators. The last stretch of path is usually under water but there is no danger and only your feet will get wet.

Tram Road   M

24.1 km (15 miles), 6 hours

Begins and ends at the Shark Valley Visitor Center. A long and usually sunny trail which follows the small, circular paved road (closed to traffic) leading, by way of Shark Valley, to a tall observation tower which can be climbed free of charge. Also possible by bicycle.

The vegetational cover differs according to the varied ecological and climatic conditions of the park: in the zones closest to the sea, where the salinity content is higher, mangrove swamps, perhaps more extensive than anywhere else in the world, predominate. The different species of mangrove belong to distinct botanical families. Growing alongside the red mangrove (Rhizophora mangle), pictured below, are the white mangrove (Laguncularia racemosa) and the black mangrove (Avicennia nitida), as well as the button mangrove (Conocarpus erectus).

BISCAYNE NATIONAL UNDERWATER PARK

Access: East of the Everglades National Park; the Visitor Center is at Homestead, a few kilometers from the Everglades main entrance.
Points of interest: This is the largest and most recently instituted underwater park (more than 700 km²/270 sq. miles) in the United States. It preserves a fine example of a coral reef, which can be visited in glass-bottomed boats, by guided scuba dives, hired canoes or organized mini-cruises. The park is open from 8 am to sunset and entry is free.

CORKSCREW SWAMP WILDLIFE SANCTUARY

Access: 90 km (56 miles) northwest of Everglades City, by State Highways 29 and 846.
Points of interest: This reserve (photograph below), owned by the National Audubon Society, is one of the most famous nature zones in the world, extending over 44 km² (17 sq. miles) to protect what remains of the Big Cypress Swamp, an area of wetland where the oldest trees in the eastern United States grow. These are swamp cypresses 40 m (130 ft) tall and 700 years old, constituting a typical habitat which has all but vanished from

Florida. The area is served by a trail 1.8 km (about 1 mile) long, entirely over raised walkways, which, if you read the accompanying guide as you go, offers the opportunity of seeing these trees and also other very rare plants and animals. By visiting this reserve after the Everglades National Park, you can successfully complete a tour through all the different natural environments of Florida. There is an entry charge.

BIG CYPRESS NATIONAL PRESERVE

Access: The area (pictured opposite) is crossed by Interstate 41 (Tamiami Trail) and by the parallel State 84 (Alligator Alley).
Points of interest: This is a vast area bordering the Everglades National Park to the north, set up to protect the park more effectively. The preserve, of great interest to nature-lovers, is crossed by the Florida Trail, a walk that covers the entire peninsula from north to south. The stretch between Alligator Alley and Tamiani Trail, over 50 km (31 miles), is described in the interesting guide by Mike and Pat Toner entitled *Florida by Paddle and Pack*, Banyan Books Ed., together with another very interesting botanical trail, Faka-hatchee Strand (17 km/10¾ miles outward only, 5½ hours). This one runs through the only mixed cypress and palm forest in Florida where forty-four different species of orchid can be found.

MONTANA

GLACIER
NATIONAL PARK

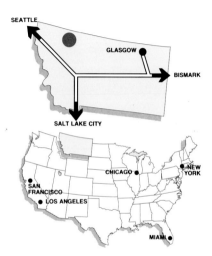

Glacier National Park is one of the world's most important nature reserves and was recognized as such by the international scientific community in 1974. It protects the northernmost extremity of the Rocky Mountains, a vast mountain region which contains more than 2,000 alpine lakes, fifty small glaciers, about 1,500 km (940 miles) of rivers and streams, extensive forests and thousands of animal species, including the grizzly bear.

The exceptional beauty of these mountains, which climb to 3,190 m (10,463 ft) at Mount Cleveland, together with the extraordinary variety of their flora and fauna, has been combined with the stunning bordering area of Waterton Park in Canada to make up the Waterton-Glacier International Peace Park.

Address: Superintendent, Glacier National Park, West Glacier, Montana 59936, tel. (406) 888-5441.
Area: 4,140 km² (1,600 sq. miles).
Altitude: From 961 m (3,152 ft) to 3,190 m (10, 463 ft) above sea level.
Access: The West Entrance is on US 2; the eastern entrances (Two Medicine Entrance, St Mary and Many Glacier Entrance) are on US 89.
Opening times: Open all year round, 24 hours a day.
Entry charge: $5 per car or $2 per person on public transport, bicycle, etc. Golden Eagle Passport valid.
Parking: Many car parks; some difficulty in summer at Logan Pass.

Glacier, former territory of the Blackfoot

So far no traces have been found of the people who are presumed to have lived here in prehistoric times. The first reliable historic evidence, therefore, goes back no further than 1792, the year in which an agent of the Hudson Bay Company reached the Glacier region after travelling southwest through Canada. At that time the warlike Blackfoot Indians were undisputed masters of the prairies of northern Montana and their dominance extended to the Glacier mountains. This huge mountainous territory, of no interest to the Blackfoot whose lives depended on the great herds of bison, had become the refuge of certain tribes, such as the Kutenai, the Kalispel and the Flathead, scattered over the wide plains. In less than a hundred years, however, the scourge of whiskey

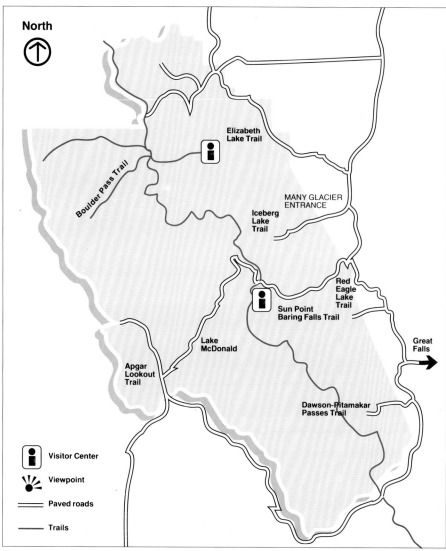

North

Elizabeth Lake Trail

Boulder Pass Trail

MANY GLACIER ENTRANCE

Iceberg Lake Trail

Red Eagle Lake Trail

Sun Point Baring Falls Trail

Lake McDonald

Great Falls

Apgar Lookout Trail

Dawson-Pitamakar Passes Trail

i Visitor Center

\\!/ Viewpoint

═══ Paved roads

─── Trails

Fuel: Service stations are in towns near the park.
Roads: Going-to-the-Sun Road is the main paved road which crosses the park from West Entrance to St Mary (open end May to mid October). Other roads, most of them dirt roads, serve many campgrounds (but are only open in summer). In the winter only the stretch of Going-to-the-Sun Road from West Entrance to Lake McDonald Lodge is negotiable.
Shops: General stores at Apgar,

Lake McDonald, Swiftcurrent, Rising Sun and Two Medicine.
Accommodation: Hotels, motels and chalets in many places in the park (see *Useful Advice*) and in nearest towns (West Glacier, Hungry Horse, Whitefish, Kalispell, East Glacier Park, Browning and St Mary).
Visitor Center: At St Mary (Open end May to mid October) and at Logan Pass (mid June to mid September); an Information Center is open all year round at Apgar.

Viewpoints: Many along Going-to-the-Sun Road.
Guided tours: In high season.
Other activities: Mountain- and rock-climbing, cross-country skiing, expeditions on horseback, by bicycle and kayak. A list of private tour operators can be obtained from the Superintendent.
Beware of: The usual perils of touring in high mountains (sudden weather changes, falling stones, cracks in ice, etc.); grizzly bears.

and the disappearance of the bison combined to mark the end of the Indians who left the region in the hands of the white man.

Hunters, gold prospectors and railroaders

In the second half of the nineteenth century Americans began to visit the Glacier region in increasing numbers, following the demise of the Blackfoot. The area attracted in particular fur trappers and prospectors for gold and other minerals, who hoped to open up new territories to their activities. Here, as happened in many other parts of the New World, there were insistent rumours, which proved totally unfounded, of rich finds, destined to lead astray innumerable groups of men who journeyed in search of a fortune. Meanwhile the area was also being surveyed by engineers of the Great Northern Railroad, who in 1889 chose Marias Pass as the route over the mountains for the railroad. After only two years the service was inaugurated and this helped enormously to open up the entire Glacier region. Visitors began to come in ever-increasing numbers, soon attracting the interest, too, of ex-prospectors and ex-hunters who saw the chance of good profits. Glacier quickly became popular and it was not long before conservationists began their campaign to win round public opinion and politicians to the idea of setting up a protected area, a proposal already put forward in 1874. However, the act instituting the National Park was only signed in 1910, thanks above all to the end of mineral-seeking activities (in fact operations in the zone had turned out to be a fiasco).

After that the park underwent a series of improvements, based on the needs of scientists and conservationists. In 1933 the Going-to-the-Sun Road was opened, running through the park from west to east, opening it up to motor vehicles and thus to large numbers of tourists. The old chalets built along the trails, which could be negotiated either on horseback or on foot, were mostly demolished, while new tourist developments sprang up along the main road and on the boundaries of the protected area. Visitors today need no additional enticement and are invited to experience the natural beauties of Glacier National Park, trekking on foot or horseback down the Going-to-the-Sun Road which retains its charm and appeal as an ideal introduction to the park.

USEFUL ADVICE

For detailed information about the many kinds of accommodation in the park, as well as advance booking (strongly recommended in summer), you need to contact Glacier Park Inc., which has two separate addresses: East Glacier Park, Montana 59434, tel. (406) 226-5551, from 15 May to 15 September, and Greyhound Tower, Station 5185, Phoenix, Arizona 85077, tel. (602) 248-6000, from 15 September to 15 May. For advance booking at Granite Park Chalet and Sperry Chalet, accessible only on foot, apply instead to Belton Chalets Inc., Box 188, West Glacier, Montana 59936, tel. (406) 888-5511.

The presence of bears, especially grizzly bears, can be a serious problem for trekkers, not so much because they are ferocious beasts but because their behaviour is sometimes hard to predict. In fact, although the bears prefer to avoid encounters with humans, they are liable to attack if they are taken by surprise or feel themselves threatened. Recent statistics show that thirty-five bear attacks have been reported, six of which have proved fatal.

These figures should not cause undue alarm because attacks by grizzly bears constitute only 3 per cent of fatal occurrences recorded inside the park between 1913 and 1981, as against 11 per cent for road accidents and 12 per cent for heart attacks. However, it is worth bearing in mind that in the innermost parts of the park an encounter with a grizzly is not all that improbable and it is best to be prepared, physically and mentally. To be on the safe side it is a good idea to make some noise while walking (a cow-bell or a can with a few stones in it will do the trick) or to sing in order to scare off the bears when they are still some distance away. In any event, it is best to avoid going out walking alone. Finally, remember that a grizzly bear, *as a rule*, cannot climb trees, so as a last resort you could escape up the nearest tree.

CLIMATE

Some very interesting climatic conditions can be found inside Glacier National Park. In addition to the variations according to altitude, typical of all mountain areas, there is a marked difference between the western and eastern sectors, determined by the presence of the line of mountain ridges, known as the Continental Divide, which runs the whole length of the North American continent. What happens is that the mass of warm, moist air coming from the Pacific and heading eastwards has to cross the Rocky Mountains which stand in its path; this causes most of the humidity to fall as rain over the western slopes, while warm, dry winds then sweep down the eastern side. Consequently in the eastern sector of the park there is less rain than in the west: the annual average is 460 mm (18 in) in the East as against 710 mm (28 in) in the West. The principal feature of the climate, however, is the snow, which can fall in any month of the year, although in July and August it is not such a common occurrence.

These two months are also the hottest, with average maximum temperatures of 26°C (79°F), and 25°C (77°F) and a minimum of 8°C (47°F) and 7.7°C (46°F) respectively. They are also the sunniest and driest months, despite frequent storms. The coldest month, on the other hand, is January, with temperatures always below zero centigrade, and the highest incidence of snowfall. This brief survey shows clearly that the climate of Glacier is typically alpine, with short summers and long, snowy winters.

Stories of rock, water and ice

Glacier is an ideal place not only for seeing mountains fashioned by the great Quaternary glaciers but also some of the most ancient rocks in the U.S.A. These are sedimentary rocks (sandstone, clay and limestone) which date back more than 2,000 million years, before the appearance of land plants and animals on the planet and when the atmosphere was still saturated with carbon dioxide. About 60 million years ago, these rocks assumed their present position during movements of the earth's crust which originated the Rocky Mountains, as demonstrated by clearly visible faults and slips in the northern sector of the park. In the course of the last 2–3 million years various major glaciations followed one another, during which a thick layer of ice covered even the Glacier area. Huge tongues of ice then slipped into the canyons dug out by ancient rivers, becoming wider and deeper until they were transformed into

immense valleys with the typical transverse U-shaped outline that we can see today. The present appearance of Glacier, therefore, is caused above all by these glaciers, the last of which thawed about 10,000 years ago, leaving behind sharp ridges, smooth rocks, innumerable lakes and huge moraines. Today's small glaciers, on the other hand, are not the remains of the Quaternary glaciers but were formed more recently; and although they are now in a regressive phase there is always a possibility that one day, should the climate again get colder, they could create new rivers of ice.

Marked trails

Glacier Natural Park has been described as the hiker's park, and in fact it is crisscrossed by more than forty marked trails for a total distance of about 1,300 km (812 miles). Only a few are discussed here, subdivided into short walks, long hikes and treks; for

PICNIC AREAS AND CAMPGROUNDS

There are properly equipped picnic areas at Apgar, Rising Sun, Sprague Creek, Many Glacier, Two Medicine and Walton Ranger Station.

Of the thirteen organized campgrounds, six are situated along the dirt road which runs from West Entrance northwards along the western boundary of the park (Logging Creek, Quartz Creek, Pelebridge, Bowman Lake, River and Kintla Lake). Four lie along Going-to-the-Sun Road (West Entrance, Lake McDonald, Avalanche and Rising Sun), and the other three are in the eastern sector (Swiftcurrent, Cut Bank and Two Medicine). The charge varies from $5 to $7 per night according to the facilities and services provided. All are only open in the summer and no advance bookings are accepted.

Free camping for overnight stops during longer treks is only permitted in particular areas: there are sixty-five scattered throughout the park. Permits must be obtained from the Ranger Stations or Visitor Centers.

On pages 138 and 139: along Going-to-the-Sun Road visitors can admire Lake St Mary, the snow-covered peaks which overlook it and the lines of Douglas fir that extend down to its shores.

The icy waters of the thawing Sperry glacier seep into the rocks, forming a network of brooks and streams.

TWO ANIMALS THAT SYMBOLIZE THE PARK

Of all the many animals in the park, two are of special interest: the mountain goat and the grizzly bear.

The mountain goat (*Oreamnos americanus*), pictured below, is a typical member of the Bovidae with a completely white coat, a prominent "beard" and small, slightly curved horns. Extremely agile and an excellent rock-climber, this large goat lives on the steep slopes at the lower limit of the perpetual snowline. It can move around without difficulty, despite its weight of up to 135 kg (300 lb), thanks to the particular form of its hooves. It is active mainly by day and usually gathers in small groups of under ten individuals to browse the alpine plants that constitute its diet. In winter it moves above the treeline but always remains within an area of some 5–10 km (3–6 miles) diameter. Mating occurs from October to December among animals of over two and a half years, the age of sexual maturity. The females give birth in May and June to one, two, and occasionally, three young. In the wild the mountain goat may live for more than twelve years, its survival being dependent more on its resistance to the harsh conditions rather than predators.

Occupying in North America the same ecological niche as the ibex (*Capra ibex*) in the Alps, it is found in the western states of Canada and only in a few national parks of the northwestern United States. One of these, of course, is Glacier National Park where its presence can be detected here and there all over; yet although it is an inquisitive animal and not particularly shy by nature, it is hard to spot or approach. There are, however, several vantage points where it can be observed and photographed, the most popular certainly being Gunsight Point.

The grizzly bear (*Ursus horribilis*), pictured right, on the other hand, has a terrible reputation, which is not entirely justified. This animal, in fact, is not a professional killer or a ferocious predator but a skilful hunter which feeds on fruit, grass, insect larvae, small mammals, salmon (particularly those that it finds lying moribund in shallow water after returning upriver) and indeed anything else edible. Its reputation for violence is derived above all from the spontaneous attacks made by females with cubs or individuals which feel themselves in some way threatened, whereas normally the bears will avoid people when they see them from afar.

Today the grizzly bear is regarded as an endangered species: its distribution area grows smaller with every passing day and is already restricted to Alaska and western Canada. In the U.S.A. it survives only in Yellowstone and Glacier National Parks, though formerly it also lived in the Sierra Nevada, as indicated by the Indian name "Yosemite" which literally means "some grizzlies may be killers." Inside Glacier the population of these huge bears is thought to be around two hundred and seems to have remained stable for several years, but none the less problems of protection are serious as a result of excessive human pressure on the ecology of the whole habitat.

At this point it may be helpful to mention briefly the bodily features which distinguish the grizzly bear from the smaller and less dangerous black bear, the only other species of bear inhabiting this park. The colour of the fur varies in the grizzly from a fawny-yellow to a dark almost black, brown. The body is very solid, with a characteristic hump on the front shoulders, the snout is rounded and the claws of the front feet are long and striking. If any uncertainty should remain after observing these features, recourse can

be had to another infallible method which dates from the earliest research on bears: aim a kick at the bear's backside and skim up a tree as quickly as you can. If the bear climbs up after you, it is a black bear: if it just bashes itself against the tree, it is a grizzly!

Grizzlies prefer to venture out around dusk, although they may be active at virtually any time of the day or night. They lead a solitary life moving around alone, except in the case of females with cubs. In spite of their weight (those in Glacier National Park weigh on average around 270 kg/600 lb), they are very agile and can run rapidly for long distances. They spend the winter hibernating inside a lair dug for that purpose. In Glacier Park, grizzlies resume full activity in April, although their winter sleep may be interrupted frequently. The sexually mature females, having mated in June, give birth in January inside their winter shelters.

Normally two cubs are born, although births of triplets are not uncommon and even cases of quadruplets have been recorded. The cubs remain with their mother until their second year, which means that many females reproduce only once every three years after weaning their young.

FLORA

The vegetational cover is dominated by
the forests. Like all mountainous areas,
however, this sector of the Rocky
Mountains also displays distinct altitudinal belts, with increasing height determining the change in environment.
From about 1,000 m (3,300 ft) upwards
the Transition Zone is characterized, in
the eastern part of the park, by extensive prairies, followed at greater heights
by forests of quaking aspen (*Populus
tremuloides*). In the wetter western
part, the yellow pine (*Pinus ponderosa*)
grows freely around the edges of the
prairie zone. Between 1,500 m (5,000 ft)
and 2,000 m (6,500 ft) the Transition
Zone gives way to the Canadian Zone or
Montane Zone, where dense and sometimes impenetrable forests encircle all
the peaks of the park. The most widely
distributed tree is the lodgepole pine (*P.
contorta*), which despite its name may
grow to a height of 24 m (80 ft) and
which forms almost pure communities
that stretch for hundreds of square kilometers. According to the type of soil,
this pine associates with other conifers,
such as the western larch (*Larus
occidentalis*) which, like all other rep-
resentatives of the genus, loses its
needles in the autumn, the western
white pine (*P. monticola*), the Douglas
fir (*Pseudotsuga menziesii*) and the
western red cedar (*Thuja plicata*), all
tree of large dimensions.

Over about 2,200 m (7,200 ft) the
harsh environmental conditions impose
a drastic limitation on tree growth. This
belt, the Hudsonian Zone, is notable for
the presence of isolated and twisted
specimens of whitebark pine (*P. albicaulis*), alpine fir (*Abies lasiocarpa*) and
alpine larch (*Larix lyallii*).

Higher still, above the treeline, is the
Arctic-Alpine Zone which remains
under snow for more than ten months of
the year. Predominant plants are shrubs
and grasses typical of the tundra, such as
the paintbrush (*Castilleja* sp.) pictured
here.

those routes requiring over a day's walking, you must obtain a permit from the ranger or from the Visitor Centers, where the appropriate maps are also available. For overnight stays, apart from the free camping areas, there are two lodges: Sperry Chalet and Granite Park Chalet.

The lengths of time and distances mentioned for the various trails include the outward and return journeys, if not otherwise specified.

Finally, before setting out on a long trek, do not forget to get information on the condition of the trails and the possible presence of grizzly bears.

SHORT WALKS

Running Eagle (Trick Falls)   E

1 km (½ mile), 30 minutes

Begins at Two Medicine Road, just north of the bridge over Two Medicine Creek; ends at Trick Falls. A very short trail which runs through a forest of spruce, including Engelmann spruce (*Picea engelmannii*) and leads to a series of waterfalls, the Trick Falls.

Cedars Trail   E

1.6 km (1 mile), 45 minutes

Begins at Going-to-the-Sun Road, north of the entrance to Avalanche Campground; ends after crossing Avalanche Creek. The trail takes its name from the tall red cedars that form one of the loveliest groves in the park.

Sun Point/Baring Falls Trail   E

2.6 km (1½ miles), 1 hour

Begins at the Sun Point parking area; ends at Baring Falls.

The trail skirts the northern shore of the St Mary Lake and goes as far as the falls. A short diversion leads to Going-to-the-Sun Point, from where there is a fine view of some of the park's highest peaks.

Rainbow Falls Trail   E

3 km (1¾ miles), 1½ hours

Begins at the jetty at the southern tip of Waterton

Lake; ends at Rainbow Falls. Relaxing walk along
the Waterton River, in one of the park's most interesting wildlife areas.

Swiftcurrent Lake Trail   E

4.2 km (2½ miles), 2 hours

Begins at the picnic area at the Many Glacier Campground; ends at Many Glacier Hotel. The trail runs
beside Swiftcurrent Lake, with a splendid view of
Mount Gould and the Grinnell and Salamander
glaciers.

Hidden Lake Overlook Trail   E

4.8 km (3 miles), 2½ hours

Begins at the Logan Pass Visitor Center (2,031 m/
6,662 ft), along Going-to-the-Sun Road; ends at
Hidden Lake Overlook. The trail, perhaps the most
popular, winds through typical alpine meadows,
climbing the ridge of the Continental Divide up to
the viewpoint over the surrounding peaks.

Avalanche Lake Trail   M

9 km (5½ miles), 4 hours

Begins at the Avalanche Campground; ends at Avalanche Lake. Pleasant walk through woods to the
western shore of Avalanche Lake.

LONG HIKES

Iceberg Lake Trail   M

15.3 km (9½ miles), 6 hours

Begins at the Swiftcurrent Campstore; ends at
Iceberg Lake. The first 4 km (2½ miles), to Ptarmigan Falls, coincides with the Ptarmigan Trail, then
descends towards Iceberg Lake, so called because of
the blocks of ice which float on its surface even at the
height of summer. Beware of grizzly bears.

Grinnell Glacier Trail   M

16.7 km (10½ miles), 600 m (1,968 ft) change in
elevation, 6½ hours

Begins at the picnic area on Many Glacier Road,
between the hotel and the campground; ends at the

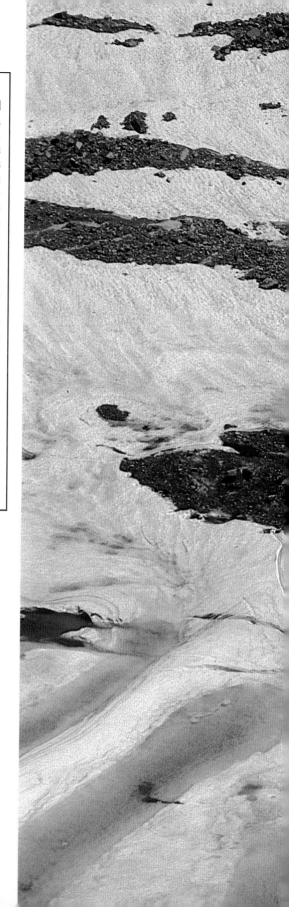

PHOTOGRAPHIC HINTS

The landscape of the Glacier National Park is dominated by whites and greens, two very bright colours in the spectrum. In composing a picture, therefore, you need to measure the light carefully as correct readings for the green will give overexposed whites and correct readings for the white will again give too much light contrast. It is better to choose a portion of landscape entirely covered with snow as a background and fill the frame accordingly taking an exposure from the subject, or to choose a uniform green backdrop and shoot the snow.

To avoid too much monotony of any one colour, take a contrasting foreground subject – flowers or lichens, or perhaps an animal belonging to one of the more trusting species. You can usually obtain variety in your photographs by including detailed close-ups of items that are of special structural interest, such as the flora, the snow and ice. Finally, a good macro lens is invaluable for detailed pictures of flowers while use of a polarized filter will successfully capture the contrasts of clouds against the blue sky.

On pages 146 and 147: the best way to see the park is to travel about on foot, making short walks from the Logan Pass Visitor Center, below Mount Wilbur.

Telephoto lenses can be used to take marvellous photographs which concentrate on small areas of natural scenery: by carefully balancing the various masses of colour and incorporating both straight lines and curves, it is possible to bring out the intricate texture of the landscape.

SOUTHWESTERN VALLEYS

This area of the park, crossed by Nyack Creek, Coal Creek and Park Creek, is by far the wildest and is excellent trekking country. There are a few trails which are only subject to maintenance work at irregular intervals so they are not nearly as well signposted as others in the park. They mostly run alongside streams and pose no special difficulties of orientation. In this sector, although you always need a permit to camp overnight, you do not have to pitch your tent in particular areas. The trail that follows the course of the Nyack Creek and crosses many passes, including Cut Bank and Dawson Pass, is highly panoramic and of great historical interest. From here, in fact, the Indians set out on their travels back and forth across the vast prairies inhabited by bison.

Many bears live in this part of the park and you must remember to keep a look out for them. Moreover, at certain times of the year the ground, which is densely covered by bushes, becomes muddy so that walking is more difficult.

foot of the Grinnell glacier. The trail runs alongside Swiftcurrent Lake and Josephine Lake, ending on the terminal moraine of the biggest glacier in the park. In summer this hike is accompanied daily by nature guides. Recommended period: end July.

Highline Trail   M

18.7 km (11¾ miles) outward only, 7 hours

Begins at the car park of the Logan Pass Visitor Center; ends at the "The Loop" on Going-to-the-Sun Road. For the first 11.5 km (7¼ miles) the trail runs parallel to the Continental Divide as far as the Granite Park Chalet (for overnight stays a permit is required and advance booking is advised), and then continues down westwards through alpine meadows full of flowers and wild animals (mountain goats and bighorns). Recommended period: mid July.

Lower and Middle Quartz Lakes Trail   D

21 km (13 miles), 640 m (2,099 ft) change in elevation, 1/2 days

Begins and ends at the Bowman Lake Campground. A strenuous circular trip through grizzly bear territory, comprising dense forests, lakes and mountain ridges. Proceeding in an anticlockwise direction, you first climb 340 m (1,115 ft) up to Quartz Ridge and then descend to Lower Quartz Lake (overnight camping possible), continuing in the direction of Middle Quartz Lake. Here there is a climb of about 300 m (985 ft) to Cerulean Ridge leading to the final descent towards Bowman Lake.

TREKS

Red Eagle Lake Trail   M

22.5 km (14 miles), 2 days

Begins at the St Mary Ranger Station; ends at Red Eagle Lake. Initially, for about 6 km (3¾ miles) it follows an old road closed to traffic. The lake, which is the trek's destination, teems with fish.

Dawson-Pitamakan Passes Trail   D

28 km (17½ miles), 2/3 days

On pages 152 and 153: strata of sedimentary rock.

Strenuous circular trek which begins and ends at the

FAUNA

The numerous types of habitats, which form a vast mosaic throughout the park, harbour a rich variety of animals, including many species of ungulate. The wooded areas with lakes, ponds and streams are the home of the elk (*Alces alces*), often seen with its muzzle in the water, feeding on its favourite aquatic plants. The mule deer (*Odocoileus hemionus*) enjoys a much wider distribution area, from conifer forests to lowland plains, while the related white-tailed deer (*O. virginianus*) prefers the forests. The wapiti (*Cervus canadensis*) is abundant but more elusive than the last species, forming herds that frequent thin woodland and, in summer, alpine meadows. Higher up, large herbivores are represented by the mountain goat (*Oreamnos americanus*) and the bighorn (*Ovis canadensis*); the latter species, once fairly common all over the western United States, is nowadays found only in three protected areas: Glacier National Park, Yellowstone National Park and Death Valley National Monument.

There are innumerable rodents, including the beaver (*Castor canadensis*), the hoary marmot (*Marmota caligata*), common in stony areas at high altitude and easily identified by its shrill alarm whistles, and various species of squirrels

and wild mice. These small mammals constitute the main source of food for the marten (*Martes americana*), a medium-sized nocturnal mustelid that lives mainly in trees. Among the notable carnivores are the black bear and the grizzly bear, the coyote, the puma (now rare) and the wolf (*Canis lupus*), which only occasionally ventures into the park from neighbouring Canada.

More than 200 bird species have been counted, many of which are aquatic, such as the Canada goose (*Branta canadensis*), the mallard (*Anas platyrhynchos*) and the harlequin duck (*Histrionicus histrionicus*). Especially characteristic of mountainous zones are various grouse: the white-tailed ptarmigan (*Lagopus leucurus*), which does not abandon the alpine meadows even in winter, the blue grouse (*Dendragapus obscurus*) and the spruce grouse (*Canachites canadensis*), photographed below, whose habitat consists of the dense forests of the Canadian Zone.

Finally, a note for birdwatching enthusiasts: every autumn, from October to December, more than 350 bald eagles (*Haliaeetus leucocephalus*) congregate along the lower course of the McDonald Creek to feed on the salmon which die after returning to the river. Nothing like this can be seen anywhere else in the world.

Two Medicine Campground. At first the trail skirts the northern shore of Two Medicine Lake, then climbs across the Bighorn Basin to Dawson Pass. From here it narrows (in fact so narrow that horses are not allowed) and becomes more exposed (not recommended for those who suffer from vertigo) as far as Pitamakan Pass, and then begins the descent to Oldman Lake, close to which is a free camping area. Recommended period: mid July.

Gunsight Pass Trail   D

30 km (18¾ miles) outward only, 2 days

Begins at Jackson Glacier Overlook on Going-to-the-Sun Road; ends at Lake McDonald Lodge. A long trek at high altitude which crosses the Continental Divide at Gunsight Pass, an ideal point for seeing mountain goats. Sperry Chalet is about two thirds of the way along the trail.

Elizabeth Lake Trail   M

31.2 km (19½ miles) outward only, 2 days

Begins at the Chief Mountain customs point on State 17, on the border with Canada; ends at Elizabeth Lake. This trail climbs to Belly River, through woods of quaking aspen (*Populus tremuloides*) and open plains, as far as Elizabeth Lake in the heart of the park. From here it passes a number of trails, including the North Circle, which begins at Swiftcurrent Lodge in the Many Glacier Valley.

Packer's Roost   D

51.5 km (32¼ miles), 3/4 days

Interesting circular trail through a region populated by black bears, grizzly bears, mountain goats, marmots and many other wild animals. It is advisable to proceed in a clockwise direction, departing from Packer's Roost at "The Loop" along Going-to-the-Sun Road. Camping overnight is possible on Flattop Mountain, at Fifty Mountain and at the Granite Park Chalet or the adjacent campground, from where the return route to the departure point descends the Highline Trail for about 11 km (7 miles).

UTAH

ARCHES
NATIONAL PARK

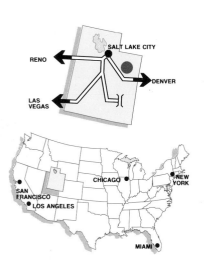

Arches National Park forms part of the huge region known as Canyonlands, which comprises southern Utah and the area north of the Colorado River. There is no other place in the world where erosion, in the course of geological eras, has so deeply incised the earth's crust as to reveal its very structure, or carved immense natural monuments, like the "arches" themselves.

In 1929 it was decided that the region should be protected so it was instituted as a National Monument. Prior to that the land had been subject to a succession of Indian cultures. About 1,000 years ago, the Anasazi and the Fremont Indians hunted the territory, but when the first colonists arrived there were only a few Ute Indians still living there. All these tribes, however, left records of themselves in beautiful, mysterious rock engravings.

Between 1830 and 1840 the area was much travelled from south to north by way of the road known as the Old Spanish Trail; and it was during those years that a certain Denis Julien, who probably explored the entire Canyonlands region, left his signature dated 9 June 1844 carved on a rock. At the end of the century a Civil War veteran named John Wesley Wolfe settled in the area of the Arches to raise cattle, living there with his family until 1910; his rather shabby ranch still exists today and can be visited.

Over the course of some forty years the original park area increased steadily in size, and eventually the National Park was inaugurated in 1971. However, there are still areas of geological interest lying outside the park so there is still scope for further growth.

Address: Superintendent, Arches National Park, PO Box 907, Moab, Utah 84532, tel. (801) 259-8161.
Area: 297 km^2 (114 sq. miles).
Altitude: From 1,200 m (3,936 ft) to 1,700 m (5,576 ft) above sea level.
Access: The only entrance to the park is on Interstate Highway 191 8.2 km (5 miles) north of Moab.
Opening times: All year round, 24 hours a day.
Entry charge: $3 per car; Golden Eagle Passport valid.
Parking: At viewpoints, Visitor Center, etc.

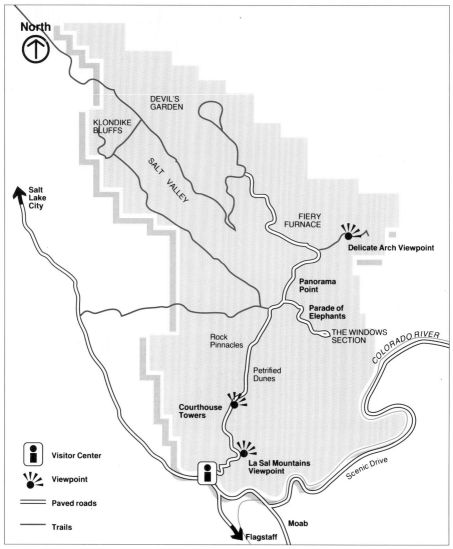

North

DEVIL'S
GARDEN

KLONDIKE
BLUFFS

SALT VALLEY

Salt
Lake
City

FIERY
FURNACE

Delicate Arch Viewpoint

Panorama
Point

Parade of
Elephants

Rock
Pinnacles

THE WINDOWS
SECTION

COLORADO RIVER

Petrified
Dunes

Courthouse
Towers

Visitor Center

La Sal Mountains
Viewpoint

Scenic Drive

Viewpoint

Paved roads

Trails

Moab

Flagstaff

Fuel: The nearest service stations are at Moab.

Roads: A single paved road of 30.9 km (19¼ miles) runs through the park from south to north; there are also a few dozen kilometers of dirt road, some reserved for off-road vehicles.

Shops: None; the nearest are at Moab.

Visitor Center: At park entrance. It is open from 8 am to 4.30 pm (in summer rather longer); closed at Christmas. It provides information, books, maps and posters;

museum on the area's geological and historical features.

Viewpoints: Many along the main road (Panorama Point, Salt Valley Overlook, etc.) and on some secondary roads (Delicate Arch Viewpoint and The Windows Section).

Guided tours: Through Fiery Furnace every day in spring and summer, accompanied by park naturalists. Other tour operators in Moab organize river trips and tours by jeep and on horseback; for information on all activities,

apply to the Visitor Center.

Other activities: In summer there are evening discussions on nature subjects at the campground. Rock climbing is permitted but only on rocks without names (consult the USGS maps or ask the rangers).

Facilities for the disabled: Easy access to the Visitor Center and public facilities on the campground.

Beware of: Crumbling rock (sandstone) especially near overhangs and ravines.

Marked trails

The park's marked trails are all alike in that none are particularly arduous, in terms of distance and change in elevation. Each one is clearly marked with heaps of stones and offers the visitor a better chance to enjoy the scenery than would be possible in a car. The following trails are described in order of distance from the Visitor Center which is situated just inside the park entrance; the times given are for the outward and return trips.

Park Avenue Trail   E

3.2 km (2 miles), 100 m (330 ft) change in elevation, 1½ hours

Begins at Park Avenue Viewpoint, about 3 km (2 miles) north of Visitor Center along the main road; ends at Courthouse Viewpoint, on the same road. This is an easy walk that crosses a canyon and is the best introduction to the geology of the park. The trail's ostentatious name, Park Avenue, is derived from the rocky "skyscrapers" which line it, like a natural cityscape.

At the northern end of the trail, there is a viewpoint over the area of Courthouse Towers, a jumble of arches, towers and hanging rocks with colourful names such as Three Gossips, Sheep Rock, Baby Arch, The Organ, etc. Morning light is best for photography, because the walls are completely in shadow in the afternoon. On the other hand, original shots of The Organ illuminated by the setting sun can be taken by zooming in with a 200 mm or 300 mm lens.

Double Arch Trail   E

0.8 km (½ mile), ½ hour

Begins at the car park at the end of the main road for The Windows, 18.8 km (11¾ miles) from the Visitor Center; ends at Double Arch. An easy walk, which takes in some of the loveliest structures in the park, such as Double Arch. The short stroll is through scenic open country with sparse clumps of Utah juniper and nut (or piñon) pine. This typical tree association gives the landscape a wholly individual appearance and illustrates the perpetual struggle for survival in desert zones.

USEFUL ADVICE

During hikes, particularly the longer and more strenuous ones, be sure to carry at least 2 pints (1 liter) of water per person in order to avoid problems of dehydration and heatstroke. Anyone who intends to camp can safely use any available water, but only after boiling it for at least two minutes; in fact chemical purifiers are useless against certain micro-organisms present in this water.

When tackling trails away from the marked itineraries you must take a map and inform the rangers where you are going; if you do get lost, it is best to wait for help rather than to waste energy by wandering around aimlessly.

During trips make sure not to damage the fragile desert soil (cryptogamic soil), which constitutes the medium of the first slow and laborious stage whereby vegetation colonizes bare rock.

CLIMATE

This is a typical desert area, with strong fluctuations of temperature, both daily and seasonal. On the hottest summer days the thermometer may rise to a maximum of 43°C (109°F), dropping rapidly after the sun goes down. The mean annual temperature is about 20°C (68°F), but during the winter this will fall to a minimum of around −8°C (18°F) and brief snowfalls may occur at high altitude. Rainfall amounts to little more than 210 mm (8¼ in) annually, mostly concentrated at the end of summer in the form of heavy showers.

PICNIC AREAS AND CAMPGROUNDS

There are three picnic areas: at the Visitor Center, at Balanced Rock and at Devil's Garden, where the paved road ends; all are equipped with tables, campfire sites and toilet facilities (with running or pool water). There is one organized campground (53 places, running water but no showers) for tents and trailers; there is no advance booking and the charge is $5 per vehicle except from November to mid March when, since there is no running water because of freezing temperatures, there is no charge. For groups of ten or more persons there are two special areas (tents only) which must be prebooked by writing to the Superintendent. Free camping around the park is regulated.

Turret Arch and The Spectacles Trail   E

1 km (½ mile), 45 m (147 ft) change in elevation, ¾ hour

Begins as Double Arch Trail (above); ends at The Spectacles. The trail is similar in character to the Double Arch one; the highlight is The Windows, the two arches known together as The Spectacles, beneath which you can have your photograph taken.

Delicate Arch Trail   E

4.8 km (3 miles), 150 m (492 ft) change in elevation, 2 hours

Begins at Wolfe Ranch, 21.7 km (13½ miles) from the Visitor Center (the last 2.9 km/1¾ miles are on a dirt road); ends at Delicate Arch. The trail crosses Salt Wash by a suspension bridge and climbs a series of natural steps to Delicate Arch, which only comes into view at the last moment.

This arch, certainly the most famous in the park, seems bigger than it really is: it is actually about 13.5 m (44 ft) high.

Sand Dune Arch, Broken and Tapestry Arch Trail   E

2.4 km (1½ miles), 1 hour

Begins at the car park at the 16-mile stone on the main road, 25.7 km (16 miles) from the Visitor Center; ends at the campground. Simple walk across broad meadows past interesting rock structures; Sand Dune Arch is especially worth seeing in the early morning when the dune, under which the foundations of the arch are buried, still bears the footprints of tiny desert animals – kangaroo rats, grey foxes, insects, etc.

Devil's Garden Trail   M/D

7.2 km (4½ miles), 100 m (330 ft) change in elevation, 5 hours, access to Fin Canyon

Begins where the main road ends, 30.9 km (19¼ miles) from the Visitor Center; ends at Dark Angel.

Of all the marked trails, this is the most strenuous and at the same time the most beautiful. Within this area, the Devil's Garden, are situated most of the arches in the park, sixty-four in number, including the Landscape Arch, which is the broadest natural rock arch in the world.

A number of paths branch off towards some of the more distant arches along the trail; there is also a path from Landscape Arch, on the right (facing in the direction of the trail), which leads across Fin Canyon and joins the trail of the Double O Arch (D itinerary). Furthermore, the Devil's Garden is perhaps the

FAUNA

The animals of the park, like the plants, are perfectly adapted to the arid conditions in which they live.

The kangaroo rats (*Dipodomys* spp.), for example, manage to survive without drinking, utilizing the water contained in seeds, which they consume thanks to the special metabolism of the kidneys, which enables them to expel highly concentrated urine. The spadefoot toad (*Scaphiopus* spp.), on the other hand, survives periods of drought and frost by burying itself in the mud to a depth of some 20 cm (8 in).

The creatures which appear least sensitive to the harsh conditions are the birds, so much so that it is not uncommon to see a golden eagle hunting rabbits in the middle of the day.

In the desert, however, animals come to life mainly at night. This is when predators, large and small, go hunting. The puma tracks down the mule deer, the grey fox searches for rodents and small birds, the rattlesnake waits for a mouse to stray within range, and the opportunistic coyote feeds on practically anything.

THE FINEST NATURAL ARCHES IN THE WORLD

Within the area under the confines of the park there are more than 200 natural arches. Many others are probably still waiting to be discovered, given that some zones even today have hardly been explored. The dimensions of these strange rock structures are very varied, the smallest being only about 1 m (3 ft) wide and the largest – the gigantic Landscape Arch – 89 m (292 ft) wide and 32 m (105 ft) high. Furthermore, the arches vary not only in size but also in form. Some arches are in pairs, like Double Arch, some are attached to long rock walls, and others, like the famous Delicate Arch, rear up in isolation.

The story of these marvels of natural engineering goes back a long time. The process, in fact, originated some 300 million years ago when the waters of an ancient sea that once covered the zone evaporated, leaving behind a layer of salt several thousands of meters thick. Subsequently over millions of years, the salt was buried under a blanket of detritus, consisting principally of sands deposited by rivers and wind, about 1.5 km (1 mile) thick. Complex geological events then transformed these sands into hard, heavy rock which crushed the salt underneath, causing fractures, movements, liquefaction and partial recrystallization. All this made the entire mass of overlying rock strata unstable, and in some areas these sank, creating huge depressions which today appear as broad valleys, whereas in others they merely cracked. Fractures such as these let in water, ice and, to a lesser extent, wind, all of which attacked the rock and initiated the slow process of erosion. With the long passage of time, the arches, as we see them today, were formed, yet they represent only a passing phase in the evolution of the landscape; in fact, the eroding processes which created them are still active and will very soon, in geological terms, bring about their complete destruction.

WOLFE RANCH AND DELICATE ARCH

About 19 km (12 miles) from the Visitor Center a dirt road leads to Wolfe Ranch (photograph below) and the Delicate Arch Viewpoint.

Visiting what remains of the ranch of John Wesley Wolfe is like taking a step back into the past, to the year 1888 when, with his son Fred, he arrived here from Ohio. It is difficult to understand what induced Wolfe to settle here and live for twenty years raising cattle on this impoverished pasture land.

Beyond Wolfe Ranch the dirt road continues for 2 km (1¼ miles) to the viewpoint over Delicate Arch. This, certainly the most famous arch in the park, is so named because of the delicate equilibrium by which it is supported. The arch is all the more remarkable for its splendid backdrop – the snowclad peaks of the La Sal Mountains.

There is a track from Wolfe Ranch which will take you to right underneath the arch.

Spectacular photographs of Delicate Arch can be taken at dawn and at sunset: in the morning you can fit in the whole arch against the broad open background, and in the evening the sun also illuminates the rocky amphitheater below the arch. A wide-angle lens will capture the enormity of the arch to maximum effect.

place for the best photographs, especially if you have the time and patience to wait until the last rays of the setting sun turn the rocks deep red.

Tower Arch Trail   M

4.8 km (3 miles), 2 hours

Begins at the Klondike Bluffs car park, 43.3 km (27 miles) from the Visitor Center (the last 14.5 km/9 miles are on a dirt road); ends at Tower Arch. This trail does not present any real difficulties but care should be taken since this is one of the wildest and least frequented sections of the park, featuring sand

THE WINDOWS SECTION

About 15 km (9½ miles) from the Visitor Center, on the right of the main road, is Balanced Rock, a huge mass of rock perched on top of a pinnacle, which seems to mount guard over the entrance to The Windows Section. This is one of the loveliest and most impressive areas, as underlined in the illustrated guide to the park, which says: "No matter how short your stay, at least go as far as The Windows Section." In fact, along this 4-km (2½-mile) stretch of road even visitors in a great hurry can admire four of the most important arches in the park (Double Arch, Turret Arch, North and South Windows). To reach them on foot, along with many other structures with exotic names such as the Parade of Elephants, see the description for Turret Arch and The Spectacles Trail.

You will not find any particular problems taking photographs of Balanced Rock, since you can wander right round it and choose the best light according to the position of the sun. Shooting into the sun can be most effective, dramatizing the structure both of the crowning rock and the pinnacle, especially if there are interesting cloud formations, such as just before a summer storm. The shape of Double Arch, on the other hand, is best revealed when the sky is slightly overcast or hazy.

dunes, clumps of pine and juniper and surrounding high rock walls.

MORE DEMANDING TRAILS

There are no other marked trails in the park so if you are interested in a trek of several days, you should purchase suitable maps and plan your own route.

For camping during treks of more than one day, as always, you will need to get a permit.

Another alternative is to follow the various dirt roads and in particular those designed for off-road vehicles, which are very suitable for hiking too.

Balanced Rock is one of nature's miracles: its balance is so precarious it looks as though it could topple at any moment.

On pages 164 and 165: on Park Avenue the rock formations are reminiscent of the characteristic lines of skyscrapers in New York.

FLORA

The plant cover is dominated by the sparse thickets of nut (or piñon) pine (*Pinus edulis*) and Utah juniper (*Juniperus osteosperma*) which cover almost half of the park's surface. Of these two plants, the juniper is more widespread because it is more tolerant of aridity and climatic conditions at low altitude (inside the park the hills do not rise to more than 1,700 m/5,575 ft in height).

The Utah juniper is recognizable by its greenish-yellow needle-like leaves and its bluish berries, used for flavouring gin; as a rule the plant has the appearance of a large shrub not more than 4.5 m (15 ft) high, with a trunk 30 cm (12 in) across. The majority of junipers normally exhibit a number of dead branches, due to a special adaptation that enables them to survive periods of intense drought, whereby the plant stops supplying water to some of its parts, sacrificing them for the benefit of the whole organism.

In rock fissures other plants supplement the pines and junipers, such as the single-leaved ash (*Fraxinus anomalus*); this species is a unique member of its genus in that instead of having big leaves composed of many leaflets, as is typical of ashes, it possesses (as its name suggests) single, leathery leaves which constitute, along with the small size of the stem, an adaptation against excessive water loss by evaporation.

In zones where the subsoil is several centimeters thick, the common blackbrush (*Coleogyne ramomissima*), pictured here, grows; this is a shrubby plant belonging to the rose family which in May and June is covered with small yellow flowers. In sandy soils of greater thickness, where water circulates deep down, the blackbrush is replaced by mediocre species of grass, as in the case of Salt Valley which, before being put under intensive pasture as it was until 1982, was covered with extensive and abundantly grassed prairies.

CASTLE VALLEY

Access: 40 km (25 miles) southeast of the park, following State 128.

Points of interest: A group of high pinnacles (Fisher Towers) at the entrance to the valley and broad grassy stretches overlooked by the snowy peaks of the La Sal Mountains, which reach a height of 3,600 m (11,808 ft).

DEAD HORSE POINT STATE PARK

Access: 51 km (32 miles) west of Moab, 43 km (27 miles) from the entrance to Arches National Park, along Interstate 191 and State 313.

Points of interest: A genuine promontory of rock facing the Colorado River, which flows 600 m (1,968 ft) below, on the border of Canyonlands National Park. It has a Visitor Center, a camp-ground, a picnic area, paths and dirt roads. An exceptional viewpoint.

CANYONLANDS NATIONAL PARK

Access: At the sector called Island in the Sky, as for Dead Horse Point State Park (48 km/30 miles from Moab).

Points of interest: 848 km² (236 sq. miles) of desert and wasteland, cut into three vast regions differentiated by the Green River and the Colorado River, which run through it: to the north is the Island in the Sky (photograph below), to the west The Maze and to the east The Needles. Hundreds of kilometers of dirt roads and trails enable visitors to explore the park, one of the wildest in the United States. Because of its enormous size there is no Visitor Center, but there are many Ranger Stations which provide information, pamphlets, maps and other material. Inside the park there are

many campgrounds (no advance booking), picnic areas and viewpoints, but no shops. The climate and the flora and fauna resemble in every way those of the Arches National Park. The address is: Superintendent, Canyonlands National Park, 125 West 2nd South, Moab, Utah 84532, tel. (801) 259-7164.

Marked trails: The following are just a few which, although of varying difficulty, present no directional problems because they are signposted throughout.

Island in the Sky District
Mesa Arch Trail, 0.8 km (½ miles), 25 m (82 ft) change in elevation, ½ hour, E; Upheaval Dome Trail, 1.6 km (1 mile), ¾ hour, E; Whale Rock Trail, 1.6 km (1 mile), 37 m (121 ft) change in elevation, 1 hour, E.

Needles District
Angel Arch Trail, 1.6 km (1 mile), 73 m (240 ft) change in elevation, 1 hour, E; Squaw and Lost Canyon Trail, 8.3 km (5¼ miles), 153 m (502 ft) change in elevation, 4 hours, M; Druid Arch Trail, 16 km (10 miles), 195 m (640 ft) change in elevation, 8 hours, M; Peek-a-boo Spring Trail, 17.3 km (11 miles), 153 m (502 ft) change in elevation, 8 hours, M; Colorado River Trail, 26 km (16¼ miles), 370 m (1,214 ft) change in elevation, 2/4 days, D.

Maze District
Horseshoe Canyon Trail, from east 5.6 km (3½ miles), 3 hours, E; Spanish Bottom Trail, 3.2 km (2 miles), 365 m (1,197 ft) change in elevation, 3½ hours, M; Pete's Mesa Trail, 9.6 km (6 miles), 30 m (98 ft) change in elevation, 4½ hours, M; Golden Stairs Trail, 35 km (22 miles), 245 m (804 ft) change in elevation, 2 days, D; North Trail Canyon Trail, 45 km (28 miles), 440 m (1,443 ft) change in elevation, 2 days, D.

UTAH

BRYCE CANYON

NATIONAL PARK

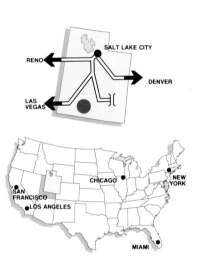

Address: Superintendent, Bryce Canyon National Park, Bryce Canyon, Utah 84717, tel. (801) 834-5322.
Area: 145 km² (56 sq. miles).
Altitude: From 2,000 m (6,560 ft) to 2,800 m (9,184 ft) above sea level.
Access: The only entrance is situated in the northern part of the park and is reached by State Highways 12 and 63.
Opening times: All year round, 24 hours a day except for the roads to Fairyland Point and Rainbow Point which close at dusk.
Entry charge: $5 per car; Golden Eagle Passport valid.
Parking: At the Visitor Center and viewpoints.

"Unka-timpe-wa-wince-pock-ich" was the name the Paiute Indians used to describe the rocky region of Bryce Canyon, which can roughly be translated as "red rocks standing like men in a bowl-shaped recess." One of their legends, in fact, told how the animals that once lived in the canyon had the power to transform themselves into humans who, as a result of their subsequent bad behaviour, were as punishment turned into rocks by a Paiute demigod named Shin-Owav.

Despite its legendary origin, the Paiute name accurately describes the physical environment of Bryce Canyon, which is not really a true canyon but a vast rock amphitheater (the area is known either as Bryce Canyon or Bryce Amphitheater), carved out and shaped by water from the side of the Paunsaugunt Plateau, another Paiute name which signifies "the beaver lodge." The nomadic Paiutes reached the area about 1,000 years after the departure of the Anasazi, an Indian tribe which inhabited an enormous region of the southwestern United States. Even today a hiker may come across an arrowhead, silent testimony to the hunting activities of the Paiute in this area.

A somewhat less magical conception of Bryce Amphitheater than is conjured up by the Indian name is the description given by Ebenezer Bryce, a Mormon settler who around 1875 came to live here and attempted to raise cattle. He defined it as "a hell of a place to lose a cow!" This probably explains why he and his wife soon abandoned the place, in 1880, in favour of the pastures of Arizona. His pioneering

Roads: A single paved road with various branch roads, for a total of 56 km (35 miles), with access to all viewpoints.

Shops: At Bryce Canyon Lodge from end May to 30 September; in nearby towns during the rest of the year.

Accommodation: At Bryce Canyon Lodge from end May to 30 September: for information and advance booking apply to TW Services Inc., 451 Main, PO Box 400, Cedar City, Utah 84720, tel. (801) 586-7686. During the rest of the year at nearby towns.

Visitor Center: On the main road 1.6 km (1 mile) outside park. It sells a variety of publications and there is a museum on the natural and historical features of the park, with audio-visual material. Closed at Christmas.

Viewpoints: The best places from which to admire the colours and shapes of the rocks are Fairyland View, Sunset Point, Inspiration Point, Bryce Point, Para View and Rainbow Point (see map).

Guided tours: The park naturalists organize many excursions, in summer and autumn and with snow-shoes in winter.

Other activities: In winter there are cross-country skiing expeditions while during the remainder of the year various tour operators organize trips on horseback lasting a few hours or a full day.

Facilities for the disabled: Easy access to the majority of buildings as well as viewpoints and the Rim Trail in the stretch between Sunrise Point and Sunset Point.

Beware of: The possibility of crumbling rock, particularly if you are with children. Along Under-the-Rim Trail and the Riggs Spring Loop there are warnings against rattlesnakes.

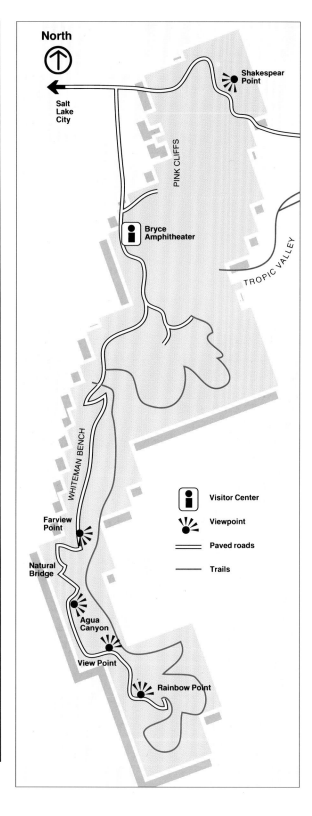

North

Salt Lake City

Shakespear Point

PINK CLIFFS

Bryce Amphitheater

TROPIC VALLEY

WHITEMAN BENCH

Farview Point

Natural Bridge

Agua Canyon

View Point

Rainbow Point

Visitor Center

Viewpoint

Paved roads

Trails

work, however, was commemorated in the name Bryce Canyon.

At the beginning of the twentieth century the first descriptions praising the forms and colours of the rocks in this area were written, and it soon became very popular. Official recognition of the fact followed quickly: on 8 June 1923 the Bryce Canyon National Monument was instituted, and a year later it was renamed Utah National Park. However, it was not until 15 September 1928 that the park doubled its area and received its present name.

Marked trails

There are 98 km (61 miles) of trails through the park, providing visitors with a chance to enjoy at close hand the shapes and colours, the plant and animal life of this region. But because the rock is so friable, it is not permitted to move off the marked trails, unless to join one of the special guided tours which are organized during the summer.

All the trails, except for the Rim Trail, begin with a more or less steep descent (See *Useful Advice* above); some of the itineraries may then be combined to make up longer treks. It should be remembered that during longer trips free camping is only allowed in the allotted areas along the Under-the-Rim Trail and the Riggs Spring Loop Trail.

The changes in elevation refer only to the climb up, while the times given apply to the outward and return journeys, except in the case of the loop trails.

Rim Trail   E

17.6 km (11 miles), 170 m (558 ft) change in elevation, 3½ hours, diversions to Boat Mesa

Begins at Fairyland Point; ends at Bryce Point (or vice versa). An easy trail, highly scenic, which skirts the rim of the plateau in which Bryce Amphitheater lies; numerous access points (North Campground, Sunrise Point, Sunset Point, Inspiration Point) make it possible to cover short stretches.

Fairyland Loop Trail   M

12.8 km (8 miles), 275 m (902 ft) change in elevation, 4½ hours

Begins and ends at Sunrise Point or at Fairyland

USEFUL ADVICE

Before setting out on an excursion, long or short, remember that because of the geographical formation of the park all trails begin with a steep descent and end with another long and tiring climb. Do not forget, either, to take with you sufficient drinking water, since for hygienic reasons it is unwise to drink any water along the way. For those on longer treks, which entail at least one overnight stop and the preparation of an evening meal, the rangers advise each person to carry 7 pints (4 liters) of water. Finally, take shelter from summer storms; lightning can always strike, especially in the higher and more exposed zones such as Boat Mesa.

CLIMATE

The altitude, always over 2,000 m (6,500 ft), has great influence on the park's climate. It is relatively colder and wetter than that of southern Utah which is generally of the desert type. From April to October days are warm, followed by very cool nights, and storms are frequent. November to March is considered as winter, with a persistent covering of snow and many days of frost. A climatic study has found that the ice-to-thaw cycle occurs more than 200 times a year, which is typical of an alpine climate. Despite this, and also because of the permeability of the rocks, surface water is not plentiful, particularly in summer.

PICNIC AREAS AND CAMPGROUNDS

The picnic areas with facilities are all situated at the viewpoints.

There are two campgrounds: North Campground and Sunset Campground, both with 230 places for tents and trailers. Each individual site has a table and cooking area and there are communal toilets and showers, the latter open only from end May to 30 September. The overnight charge is $5 per vehicle; advance booking is only accepted for organized groups.

The North Campground is a few hundred yards south of the Visitor Center, while Sunset Campground is close to Sunset Point.

Free camping is not permitted in the park. Hikers on trips that last more than a day (e.g. Under-the-Rim Trail) may only camp in particular spots and these have no facilities. There are many of them so that longer treks can be conveniently broken into daily stages.

Point. This loop trail is one of the most spectacular in the park, taking in some of the most beautiful and famous rock structures: Chinese Wall, Tower Bridge, Palace of the Fairy Queen, Ruins of Athens, etc. There are also some very old bristlecone pines growing along the trail, and in the dry zones close to Boat Mesa you may see the horned lizard. The stretch between Sunrise Point and Fairyland Point coincides with the Rim Trail.

Queen's Garden Trail   E

2.4 km (1½ miles), 100 m (328 ft) change in elevation, 1½ hours

Begins and ends at Sunrise Point. It is a fairly easy trail which crosses one of the most colourful areas of the park, the Queen's Garden. This is a rock structure which is named after Queen Victoria. When compared with photographs of twenty-five to thirty years ago, it is clear how considerable erosion has been tearing away at the "crown." Another formation along this trail is Gulliver's Castle.

Navajo Loop Trail   E/M

2.4 km (1½ miles), 160 m (525 ft) change in elevation, 2 hours

Begins and ends at Sunset Point. A delightful walk

which starts with a sharp zigzag descent and then carries on through Wall Street, a true fracture of the earth's crust, with high walls which are only about 7.5 m (25 ft) apart at some points. Another geological feature to be seen along the trail is Thor's Hammer; this mushroom-shaped pinnacle demonstrates very clearly how layers of sediment, varying in hardness, were deposited in the ancient Lake Flagstaff; here the hard top has protected the softer rock beneath from erosion. A last example of differential erosion is provided by Twin Bridges.

The Paiute Indians described the region of Bryce Canyon as that of the "red rocks standing like men in a bowl-shaped recess," and they believed that these jumbled figures were the work of an avenging god. The strange structures of the Bryce Canyon National Park do indeed bear a human appearance and many have been named accordingly; but from the geological point of view they are simply the result of 60 million years' deposition of clay and sediment and of water erosion.

Peek-a-boo Loop Trail   M

9 km (5½ miles), 250 m (820 ft) change in elevation, 4 hours, linked with Queen's Garden Trail and Navajo Loop Trail

Begins and ends at Bryce Point. A strenuous hike which leads right through the Bryce Amphitheater where you will need to consult the map to find the names of all the strange and marvellous rock structures. Among the best known are Wall of Windows, The Cathedral and Silent City. The best time to do this trek is early in the morning when long shadows create extraordinary optical effects among the pinnacles and spires. The trail is linked to others which begin and end at Sunrise and Sunset Points.

Remember to look out for horses as you go; this

VIEWPOINTS

Fairyland Point

This is the viewpoint closest to the park entrance and as such provides the best introduction to the veritable fairyland of Bryce Canyon. It is an experience not to be missed, a close-up view that makes you want to reach out and almost touch the towers and pinnacles.

Sunrise Point and Sunset Point

These two viewpoints, only some 800 m (½ mile) from each other, overlook Bryce Canyon proper. The name of the former is particularly appropriate because it is a marvellous spot for watching the sunrise. In order to see the sunset, on the other hand, you must walk a bit farther to Inspiration Point. The panorama from both viewpoints spans a distance of more than 160 km (100 miles) as far as Aquarius Plateau at an altitude of 3,000 m (9,840 ft) – the highest plateau in North America.

Agua Canyon Viewpoint

This viewpoint lies on the main road about 19 km (12 miles) from the Visitor Center, at an altitude of just under 2,700 m (8,856 ft). From here you can look at the shape of two mighty rock structures called The Hunter and The Rabbit, although it needs a bit of imagination to recognize them as such. It is a splendid panorama over one of the most colourful areas of the park, particularly vivid just after a rain shower.

Yovimpa Point and Rainbow Point

These two observation points, quite close to each other, are at the southern end of the main road, about 27 km (17 miles) from the Visitor Center, at an altitude of 2,776 m (9,105 ft), the highest spot in the park. From here you can enjoy a splendid view of the entire region as far as the Grand Canyon. The oldest bristlecone pine in the park (1,700 years) grows near Yovimpa Point.

trail can be done either on foot or on horseback and the park regulations stipulate that horses have precedence, so that walkers must move to the right and leave the trail free.

Hat Shop Trail   M

6.2 km (3¾ miles), 280 m (918 ft) change in elevation, 4 hours

Begins and ends at Bryce Point. This trail, little

frequented, constitutes the first stretch of the Under-the-Rim Trail (see below) and leads to an area crowded with pinnacles, all of which are topped by a hard rock "hat" (hence the name). Return by the same route.

Technically the canyons of this park are not canyons in the accepted sense, for they have no recognizable entry and exit points; they are simply fractures in the earth's crust.

Under-the-Rim Trail   D

35 km (22 miles), 460 m (1,509 ft) change in elevation, minimum 2 days

A FAIRYLAND

People tend to run out of adjectives trying to describe the landscape of Bryce Canyon. Even the best series of photographs cannot faithfully reproduce the astonishing shapes and colours of its rocks because they change so much according to the light (photographs below and opposite), the point of observation and the weather conditions.

It is hard to believe that the magical land of Bryce Canyon could be the result of normal chemical and physical processes, yet there is nothing exceptional about its origins.

Sixty million years ago an enormous lake, named Lake Flagstaff by geologists, covered a vast area that includes the present park. At the bottom of this inland sea – such were its dimensions – alternate layers of sand and mud accumulated to a thickness of more than 600 m (1,970 ft), which, because of the presence in the water of calcium carbonate and the action of geological phenomena, were transformed into rock. These rock strata collectively make up the so-called Wasatch Formation, better known, for its vivid coloration, as The Pink Cliffs.

During the last 25 million years, due to folding in southern Utah and northern Arizona, which led to the disappearance of Lake Flagstaff and the fragmentation of the earth's crust into plateaus, the rocks of the Wasatch Formation have remained exposed to the erosive and destructive action of water. The erosion has almost halved the thickness and is still continuing. The consequence of this action has been the fantastic forms which amaze the tourists: spires, towers, pinnacles, pagodas, human and animal figures, etc.

Yet the colour of each rock layer is a characteristic acquired at the very moment of its origin, when sand and mud were deposited on the bottom of Lake Flagstaff mixed with minute quantities of oxides of iron and manganese. The former is responsible for the reds and the latter for the various tones of blue and violet.

FLORA

The vegetation of the park, as is typical of high mountain zones, is divided into altitudinal planes or belts, caused by the climatic variations that occur with increasing height. Thus the lower belt, below 2,100 m (6,890 ft), with higher temperatures and an average of 305 mm (12 in) of rainfall per year, is notable for species which can withstand arid conditions, such as the nut pine, the Utah Juniper and the Gambel oak (*Quercus gambelii*). Between 2,100 m (6,890 ft) and 2,700 m (8,855 ft) is the belt of the western yellow pine (*Pinus ponderosa*); thanks to the rain, the vegetation of this belt is more luxuriant and consequently there is more animal life. A very common plant is the bearberry (*Arctostaphylos* spp.), also known as manzanita, a shrub which grows freely along the rims of canyons and under pines; it is easily recognized by its leaves, which stand vertical to the ground and perpendicular to the north-south axis. Over 2,700 m (8,855 ft) is the spruce, fir and poplar belt, where the bristlecone pine (*P. aristata*) also grows; this is the oldest known living organism. In the undergrowth many flowers bloom (photograph below).

Begins at Bryce Point; ends at Yovimpa Point. This long trail, for which a free permit is needed from the Visitor Center (see *Picnic Areas and Campgrounds*, page 174), runs from north to south through the oldest geological sector of the park containing a plentiful and varied range of plants and animals. Numerous side trails make it possible to make a diversion and then get back to the main road which comes from the Visitor Center. It is also possible to prolong the trail by following the Riggs Spring Loop Trail.

Riggs Spring Loop Trail M

14 km (8¾ miles), 510 m (1,673 ft) change in elevation, 5 hours

Begins and ends at Yovimpa Point. The trail is similar to the one described above only that it can be done in a single day. It includes splendid views of the Pink Cliffs. The first stretch, downhill, crosses a fine forest of yellow pines.

The repeated sequence of chemical and physical processes over millions of years have produced incredible colours in the rocks, which have taken on an astonishing diversity of shapes.

On pages 182 and 183: the layers that make up the countless columns and pinnacles are not only spectacular in colour but also of enormous geological interest.

PHOTOGRAPHIC TIPS

The fascinating pink and white calcareous rock structures of Bryce Canyon are wonderful subjects for an unlimited variety of photographs.

It is preferable to take shots of individual canyons when the sun is quite low in the sky, though not too low as, given their depth, there is a risk of taking a picture cut through diagonally by a line of shadow, with the lower part in darkness and the upper part correctly exposed. For this reason the best time for such photographs is mid morning or mid afternoon, and not around midday. For panoramic shots, because the area to be covered is so vast, you will almost certainly need to find something in the foreground to counterbalance the spatial effect and give a sense of proportion.

Telephoto lenses can be used to achieve spectacular shots of rock pinnacles in good perspective. If you take the peaks when the first rays of sunshine are on them, you can capture the dramatic effect of rows of pinnacles receding into the distance. The effect of reflection in the canyon makes the inner walls seem illuminated by powerful lights and pictures of this strange phenomenon can be extremely interesting.

Yovimpa Pass Trail E

4 km (2½ miles), 1½ hours

Begins and ends at Yovimpa Point. A pleasant and easy trail along the first stretch of the Riggs Spring Loop Trail. When you reach the Yovimpa Pass free camping area, return by the outward route.

Bristlecone Loop Trail E

1.6 km (1 mile), ½ hour

Begins and ends at Rainbow Point. A short, level, looping trail which offers splendid views of canyons and rock walls. The path goes through a forest of firs and then skirts the rim of an overhang.

FAUNA

One of the most interesting animals now living in the park, not so much for its numbers as for its changing fortunes, is the white-tailed prairie dog (*Cynomys leucurus*), an attractive rodent similar to the marmot both in appearance and in its markedly social behaviour patterns. These animals became extinct inside the park at the beginning of the 1950s as a result of being relentlessly hunted by cattle ranchers and farmers, who detested them for two reasons: the holes they dug in the ground often caused their horses to stumble, and they fed voraciously on their crops. In 1974 the National Park Service began to reintroduce the rodents, which play an important role in the ecology of their natural habitat, to the areas around the Visitor Center and the Sunset Campground. The first breeding successes were recorded in 1978 and today the population of prairie dogs in the park is considered to be numerically stable and healthy.

Many other rodents also live in the park, including three species of chipmunk (genus *Tamia*), attractive members of the squirrel family.

Among the smaller creatures of the park is the short-horned lizard (*Phrynosoma douglassi*), which can sometimes be observed basking in the sun in quiet, sheltered zones (from early August

guided tours are organized to Boat Mesa specifically to see the newly born lizards). The biggest animal is the mule deer, quite common in all the parks of the western United States. This ungulate, which gets its vernacular name from its characteristically large ears, grazes freely in fields and meadows even along the roadside, where it can most often be seen at dawn and dusk. Other large mammals which once lived in the Bryce Canyon region have, however, been less fortunate, their populations having been drastically reduced or even wiped out altogether by man. The grizzly bear and the wolf, for example, are now extinct, while the wapiti, the puma, the black bear and the bighorn are extremely rare; the restricted dimensions of the park are insufficient to guarantee the survival of these animals and the likelihood is that they too will soon disappear.

Nevertheless birds are here in abundance. From May to October some 164 species are to be seen in the park, including the golden eagle, the red-tailed hawk (*Buteo jamaicensis*), various species of woodpecker, the western tanager (*Piranga ludoviciana*), Clark's nutcracker (*Nucifraga columbiana*), pictured below, and the blue grouse (*Dendragapus obscurus*), a common inhabitant of spruce, fir and poplar forests.

ZION NATIONAL PARK

Access: The Zion Visitor Center is 138 km (86 miles) from the Bryce Canyon Visitor Center, reached by State 12, Interstate 89 and State 9 in that order. Entry charge $5; Golden Eagle Passport valid.

Points of interest: This vast protected area of 595 km² (165 sq. miles), along with Bryce Canyon and Grand Canyon, form a unique trio of natural marvels. In the rocks of these three parks, considered in the sequence Grand Canyon–Zion–Bryce, the evolution of the last 600 million years of the earth's history can be read far more drama-

tically and effectively than in any book of geology. The wild open spaces of Zion National Park are ideal for hiking and trekking, for there are plenty of marked trails, ranging from short ten-minute strolls to two-day excursions, as well as numerous off-trail routes. There is scope, too, for rock climbing, cycling, horse riding and cross-country skiing.

Dozens of miles of paved road enable visitors to reach the most spectacular viewpoints without difficulty. Facilities are provided at two Visitor Centers (Zion Canyon and Kolob Canyons), two campgrounds ($6 per night, no booking, maximum 14 days stay), a motel (Zion Lodge, open May to October, for information apply to TW

Services), and two picnic areas. For further information contact the Visitor Centers and write to or telephone the Superintendent, Zion National Park, Springdale, Utah 84767, tel. (801) 772-3256.

Marked trails: The following list includes a few of the simpler walks along marked trails. In a separate category is the Virgin River Narrows Route, a trek of 26 km (16¼ miles), amid marvellous scenery, along and through the Virgin River area, which takes a whole day (July to October only; obligatory permit from the Visitor Centers).

Weeping Rock Trail (0.8 km/½ mile, 30 m/100 ft change in elevation, ½ hour, E); Canyon Over-

look Trail (1.6 km/1 mile, 50 m/160 ft change in elevation, 1 hour, E); Emerald Pools Trail (1.9 km/1¼ miles, 21 m/70 ft change in elevation, 1 hour, E); Gateway to the Narrows Trail (3.2 km/2 miles, 1½ hour, E); Hidden Canyon Trail (3.2 km/2 miles, 260 m/850 ft change in elevation, 3 hours, M); Sand Bench Trail (5.8 km/ 3½ miles, 150 m/490 ft change in elevation, 3 hours, M); Angels Landing Trail (8 km/5 miles, 450 m/1,475 ft change in elevation, 5 hours; trail partly fitted with chains, M/D); East Rim Trail (12 km/7½ miles, 655 m/2,150 ft change in elevation, 7 hours, M); West Rim Trail (42.6 km/ 26½ miles, 1,095 m/3,590 ft change in elevation, 2 days, D).

CAPITOL REEF

NATIONAL PARK

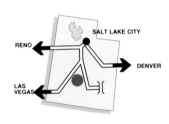

"Sleeping rainbow" is the name the Paiute Indians gave to the eastern spurs of the Waterpocket Fold, an arid, rocky region overlooked by high walls and cut by narrow, winding canyons. This is the Capitol Reef National Park which, like an impregnable rampart, rears up for a distance of some 160 km (100 miles), cutting central-southern Utah into two. The visitor's first impression is of an inhospitable region, without any life, where the only plants are a few stunted shrubs and twisted trees. Yet life does, in fact, exist here, albeit hidden in rock cracks and cavities, awaiting the cooler night hours. To travel through the park and breathe in this strange air of expectancy, which seems to pervade even the mineral world, is to be immersed in a natural environment that is truly untainted, and capable of springing continual surprises.

Indians, Mormons and . . . the park

Address: Superintendent, Capitol Reef National Park, Torrey, Utah 84775, tel. (801) 425-3791.
Area: 608 km^2 (235 sq. miles).
Altitude: From 1,200 m (3,936 ft) to 2,600 m (8,528 ft) above sea level.
Access: Either from east or west by State Highway 24.
Opening times: All year round.
Entry charge: $3 per vehicle.
Parking: At the Visitor Center, picnic areas and some viewpoints.

The Paiute Indians replaced the Fremont Indians until, in 1866, they were driven away by a group of Mormons who then settled permanently along the banks of the Fremont River early in the 1880s. The bottom of the valley contained good pasture land, the fields were irrigated by rivers and the small side valley resembled natural hothouses. Certain families founded the village of Fruita, where Sulphur Creek flows into the Fremont; and for the next eighty years these folk lived by selling fruit (peaches, cherries, apricots and pears) and occasionally driving their herds of cattle through the canyons of the Waterpocket Fold. In the 1920s some of them came together to promote the institution of a national

Fuel: There are no service stations. The nearest are in towns on the main roads.

Roads: State 24 is the only paved road. Of the dirt roads, the only easily negotiable one is the Scenic Drive (16.1 km/10 miles); for other road conditions, enquire at the Visitor Center.

Accommodation: In the towns along State 24 outside the park (Hanksville, Torrey, Bicknell, Loa).

Visitor Center: On State 24. It is open from 8 am to 7 pm in the period from 1 June to first Monday in September (Labour Day), and from 8 am to 4 pm for the rest of the year. It is closed on Thanksgiving Day (fourth Thursday in November), at Christmas and New Year. There is an information office with audio-visual material and publications on the park.

Viewpoints: Panorama Point (on State 24); Goosenecks Overlook (branch off State 24); Fremont Overlook; Rim Overlook; Brimhall Bridge Overlook (branch off Notom Road).

Guided tours: These are only available in summer. The park naturalists also give talks every evening in high season.

Other activities: Long trails for off-road bikes; private tour operators organize one-day off-trail trips and treks of several days on foot or in jeeps.

Beware of: Rivers and streams rising suddenly, especially in summer.

Facilities for the disabled: Easy access to the Visitor Center, communal facilities at campgrounds and part of the Fremont River Trail. For the blind, there are special exhibition areas at the Visitor Center and also recorded cassettes.

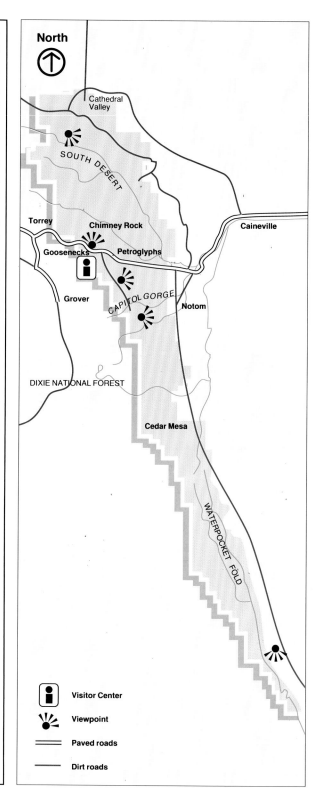

monument, both to encourage tourism and preserve the region's beauty. This came about in 1937. After that the resident population began to dwindle, while the territory gradually lost its primitive, isolated desert character as many old roads were transformed into highways. In the course of the 1960s Fruita became wholly depopulated and its orchards were abandoned. Finally, in 1971, the Capitol Reef National Park was inaugurated in order to protect the entire length of the Waterpocket Fold in its pristine state.

A world of stone

The precipitous rock walls that typify the landscape of the park are of sandstone (grains of sand of varying dimensions that are stuck together): and this is the most common type of rock throughout the zone.

These rocks are described by special names, according to the different characteristics, the surroundings in which they were formed, and their age. The sandstone is therefore classified into three different formations: Wingate, Kayenta and Navajo, like those to be found in other parts of the southwestern United States. The red colour of the walls of the Wingate Formation is unmistakable, while above them, almost like a crown, the domes and towers of the Navajo Formation rise up in a warm creamy colour. Capitol Reef, which is a part of the Waterpocket Fold, derives its name from one of the structures which bears a resemblance to the Capitol in Washington D.C. Another of these domes is called the Golden Throne.

The rocks which lie below and above the sandstone also have distinctive features. For example, the clays of the Moenkopi Formation were formed in the shallow, calm Triassic seas; they still retain today not only the prints of the primitive amphibians who once lived there but also characteristic folds known to geologists as ripple marks. These are the marks made by the wavy movements of fossils on the ocean bed.

To the east of the Waterpocket Fold are the more recent clays of the Morrison (highly coloured) and Mancos (grey) formations, which were eroded by water in a veritable labyrinth of small, dry valleys, the so-called badlands. Finally, in the northern sector of the park, where the landscape changes radically as a result of desert replacing the high walls of

USEFUL ADVICE

Even if you are only staying a few hours, it is essential to bring a sufficient supply of water because it is inadvisable to drink from pools along the way. If you want to cook at any of the campfire sites provided at the picnic areas or campgrounds, you must purchase wood or charcoal before entering the park. If you want to take photographs (for a really good series of shots, a telephoto lens of at least 300 mm is recommended), work on the principle that the best pictures can be had when the sun is low, so choose the hours of early morning and late afternoon.

CLIMATE

The Visitor Center is situated at an altitude of about 1,650 m (5,410 ft) yet, in spite of this, the temperature in summer here is high. The hottest months are June and July, with maximum temperatures above 30°C (86°F) and minimum ones around 10–15°C (50–59°F). From July to September violent summer storms can cause sudden and dangerous flooding. The desert climate of the area is somewhat cooler in spring and autumn, and turns almost cold from mid December to February, when daytime temperatures are maximum 10°C (50°F) and below zero centigrade at night. Brief snowfalls may occur at this period, but this averages less than 40 cm (16 in) a year.

The average annual rainfall level is below 180 mm (7 in). The best seasons for visiting the park are therefore spring and autumn.

PICNIC AREAS AND CAMPGROUNDS

There are three picnic areas. The first is 5 km (3 miles) east of the Visitor Center (tables, campfire sites, toilets, no drinking water); the second is 1.2 km (¾ mile) from the Visitor Center along the Scenic Drive (tables, toilets, drinking water); and the third is in the southernmost part of the park along the Burr Trail Road.

There are three campgrounds, open all year round, with no advance booking. The first is 1.6 km (1 mile) from the Visitor Center along the Scenic Drive, and well equipped (53 places with table and cooking area, two communal rooms with running and drinking water, toilets but no showers), costing $5 per vehicle. The second is at Cedar Mesa, in the southern part of the park (5 places with table, toilets, no drinking water), entrance free; and the third (no facilities) is in Cathedral Valley, entrance free. Two small areas near the main campground are reserved for organized groups and should be booked in advance. Permission is needed for free camping.

the Fold, erosion has modelled the soft sandstone of Entrada into curious "cathedrals" up to 150 m (490 ft) high.

Water for survival

The desert climate of this area creates drastic living conditions both for its plants and its animals. The Fremont River constitutes a self-contained oasis where water flows throughout the year, irrigating the old orchards and encouraging the growth of a luxuriant vegetation (poplars, willows and tamarisks) which attracts animals such as the mule deer (*Odocoileus hemionus*), the yellow warbler (*Dendroica petechia*), the leopard frog (*Rana pipiens*) and the beaver (*Castor canadensis*).

Elsewhere in the park, this happy situation prevails only in certain stretches along Pleasant Creek, Oak Creek and Lower Hall's Creek.

Marked trails

The trails described here are all well signposted and they provide the easiest introduction to the natural beauties of the park and its places of historical interest. The trails are subdivided into three geographical areas (West entrance of the park, Fremont

River and Scenic Drive). The distances and times given apply to the outward and return journeys combined, unless otherwise indicated.

WEST ENTRANCE OF PARK

Goosenecks Trail East   E

0.3 km (¼ mile), 25 minutes

Begins at Goosenecks Overlook, the viewpoint close to Panorama Point on State 24; ends at Sulphur Creek Rim. A very short and level walk which follows the east rim of Sulphur Creek canyon, 100 m (330 ft) deep, with a splendid view of the Waterpocket Fold and the Henry Mountains on the horizon, particularly impressive at sunset. Interesting erosions of the clays of the Moenkopi Formation can be seen alongside the trail.

Goosenecks Trail West   E

0.8 km (½ mile), 50 minutes

Similar to the previous walk, except that, after the viewpoint at the start, the trail takes the western rim of the canyon. You can enter Sulphur Creek Canyon and continue on foot to the Visitor Center.

The high walls of Capitol Reef stretch for a hundred miles, dividing the central-southern zone of Utah into two parts. The landscape of the park consists of vertical walls of sandstone in which three different formations may be distinguished: the sandstone of the Wingate Formation is red, that of the Navajo Formation is creamy white while the Kaienta Formation is of no colour in particular. The delicate desert vegetation contrasts vividly with the surroundings.

Chimney Rock Trail E

5.6 km (3½ miles), 165 m (541 ft) change in elevation, 2½ hours

Begins and ends at the Chimney Rock car park alongside State 24, a few hundred yards west of Panorama Point. This is a circular trail dominated by the impressive bulk of Chimney Rock; in the first stretch you can follow a fairly strenuous climb which leads to a ridge with a fine view.

You can enter Chimney Rock Canyon and walk as far as Spring Canyon, the longest of the Waterpocket Fold. This trail of 14 km (8¾ miles) is unmarked and is an excellent test run for those wanting to attempt longer off-trail treks.

FREMONT RIVER

Hickman Bridge Trail E

3.2 km (2 miles), 120 m (394 ft) change in elevation, 1½ hours

Begins at the Hickman Bridge car park to the side of

The Goosenecks canyon derives its name from the characteristic hooked shape of the rocks. This can be seen clearly from the Goosenecks Overlook, signposted a few hundred yards away from the main road which leads from Toney to the Visitor Center.

PETROGLYPHS AND FREMONT INDIANS

Pictures and rock carvings (petroglyphs) are to be found on the walls of certain canyons, representing the sophisticated culture of the Fremont Indians. They mostly depict human figures with broad shoulders and elaborate hairstyles, adorned with necklaces and earrings, and surrounded by various animals, notably the bighorn, a species of large mountain goat typical of the western United States. The significance of these forms of artistic expression is still unknown. The first certain evidence of the presence, around the Fremont River, of the Fremont Indians, dates from about A.D. 800. They were experienced farmers who cultivated a type of maize particularly resistant to drought and extremes of temperature, exploiting the short summers to the full; logically they would have supplemented this with hunting. Archaeologists have found in the park numerous stone utensils and even today, along certain trails (especially the Hickman Bridge Trail), you can see the deposits of stone and wood of the moki huts in which the Indians used to store maize, seeds and other food. The Fremont abandoned the zone around 1300 because of climatic changes which destroyed their crops and threatened their survival, and then vanished.

How to photograph the petroglyphs

The most easily accessible spot for taking photographs of petroglyphs is along State 24, not far from the Visitor Center, where there is a car park. Because the petroglyphs are under a covering, you ideally need to be there during the early afternoon as later on the rock face is in shadow. It is best to use a telephoto lens of at least 300 mm because, as a result of the crumbling of part of the wall above, you are not allowed to go beyond the barrier.

State 24, about 2.5 km (1½ miles) east of the Visitor Center; ends at Hickman Bridge. Easy walk through canyon country which leads to a point underneath Hickman Bridge, a natural bridge 40 m (130 ft) high, which provides a view of Capitol Dome and the more distant Henry Mountains. There are informative panels along the route concerning the most interesting natural aspects of the trail. You also pass Indian ruins.

Cohab Canyon Trail E

5.6 km (3½ miles), 120 m (394 ft) change in elevation, 3 hours

Begins at the campground; ends at State 24, almost

The erosive action of water has created strangely sculpted forms in the sandstone rocks of the park; the phenomenon is most clearly seen at Pleasant Creek, in the southernmost part of the marked trails.

opposite the Hickman Bridge car park. The first 240 m (260 yds) of the trail are the hardest, but a series of zigzags somewhat eases the climb into Cohab Canyon. From here the trail is fairly flat so that you can fully enjoy the delights of this small canyon excavated in the Wingate Formation sandstone, with its many grottoes and curiously eroded rock walls. The canyon owes its name to a legend which tells how Mormon cohabitationists hid here from federal agents. A series of short tracks branching off the main trail leads to viewpoints. It is also linked to the Cassidy Arch Trail and the Frying Pan Trail.

MONOCLINE

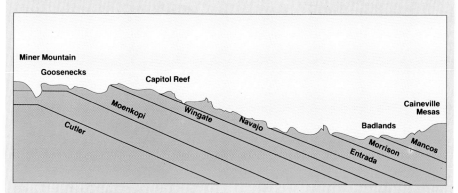

The Waterpocket Fold is one of the clearest and most spectacular examples in the world of a monocline, about 160 km (100 miles) long from north to south. The geological term "monocline" signifies a fold of the crust which connects two areas of parallel rock strata, situated at two different levels; a kind of gigantic step or, better still, gigantic chute, in which the join is inclined at an angle. This structure is easily recognizable in the Waterpocket Fold, and even its origin is known. About 70 million years ago, tremendous forces associated with continental drift and the formation of the Rocky Mountains brought about a lifting of the Colorado Plateau and numerous collateral effects, one of the most spectacular of which was the Waterpocket Fold. The rock strata which made up the plateau were formed by the accumulation of sediment and detritus in different environments – the rivers of the Permian, the muddy plains of the Triassic, the deserts of the Jurassic and the seas of the Cretaceous – and these lifted more noticeably to the west than to the east, thus creating the dipping fold.

From then on, water, ice thawing and the wind combined continuously to create canyons, pinnacles, arches, towers and strangely eroded shapes. The softest rocks were most affected by erosion and entire strata were entirely swept away. The "chute" therefore appears as a series of irregular steps, sloping from west to east, and each step represents the tip of a rock layer; the harder the rock, the higher and more vertical the walls. It is this very characteristic, immediately visible to anyone entering the park from the west, which gave the first explorers the impression of being confronted by an impassable reef.

Fremont River Trail   E/M

4 km (2½ miles), 230 m (755 ft) change in elevation, 1½ hours

Begins at the campground; ends at Fremont Overlook on Miner's Mountain. The first 800 m (½ mile) wind through orchards along the river and constitute the least strenuous part of the route, also accessible to the handicapped. Then the path becomes steeper and there is a tiring climb to the viewpoint, at a height of about 1,800 m (5,904 ft), affording a broad view over the Fremont River Canyon and the Fruita Valley, with the walls of Capitol Reef above.

Rim Overlook Trail   M

7.3 km (4½ miles), 330 m (1,082 ft) change in elevation, 4 hours

Begins at the Hickman Bridge car park; ends at Rim Overlook (viewpoint). The first stretch of 400 m (¼ mile) coincides with the Hickman Bridge Trail, then the walk becomes more energetic as the path climbs to the top of one of the largest rock spurs overlooking the former town of Fruita. From this vantage point you can get some idea of the scope of the irrigation work achieved by the first settlers. From Rim Overlook, at an altitude of more than 1,900 m (6,232 ft), you can enjoy a splendid view in all directions.

SCENIC DRIVE

Capitol Gorge Trail   E

3.2 km (2 miles), 1½ hours

Begins at the Capitol Gorge car park, at the termination of the Scenic Drive; ends at The Tanks. This easy, level trail covers the route used by pioneers with their wagons and for some eighty years it was the most important road in the state of Utah. The trail winds through a large canyon where rock carvings made by the Fremont Indians and the signatures and messages of pioneers and explorers can be seen on the walls. The marked trail comes to an end at the waterpockets known as The Tanks. Carrying on, you can quite easily reach Notom, a small town east of the park.

WATERPOCKETS

The waterpockets are natural basins where rainwater occasionally collects in summer. These pools swarm with life, exemplifying complex ecosystems in miniature where the animals are perfectly adapted to endure long periods of drought. Adult toads survive by wrapping themselves inside a sac of mucus and burying themselves deep below the crust of dry mud. The larvae of mosquitoes and other dipterans can withstand the loss of up to 92 per cent of body water. The eggs of certain tiny crustaceans (genus *Lepidurus*) can survive in the dust of a pool for up to twenty-five years, waiting for rain to fill it anew, proving a strength of resistance equal to that of the seeds of some desert plants. As a rule, however, rain does not take that long to occur.

BIZARRE ROCK FORMATIONS

It is worth visiting Twin Rocks, two almost identical rocks situated close to the western entrance of the park on State 24. They are composed of two types of rock and their strange shapes are caused by a difference in resistance to erosion. The upper parts are constituted of Shinarump conglomerate (a sedimentary rock made of small pieces of gravel and sand), which has protected the softer clay-like rock underneath (Moenkopi Formation). These same kinds of rock created many other forms in larger dimensions, such as Chimney Rock (see Chimney Rock Trail, page 194) and the Egyptian Temple, one of the major attractions of the Scenic Drive on which it is found. This dirt road, always open to ordinary vehicles, provides visitors, even if short of time, with an excellent idea of the typical park landscape and is strongly recommended.

Impressive rock structures of soft sandstone and hard conglomerates are overlooked by The Castle.

Pleasant Creek   E

9.6 km (6 miles), 4 hours

Begins at Sleeping Rainbow Ranch; ends at Notom. The trail follows the course of Pleasant Creek, which flows all year round, for half the way through Capitol Reef and for the other half across open country to Notom.

This trail is unmarked but is to be recommended because it is an easy walk through attractive scenery, and includes some rock carvings.

Grand Wash Trail   E

7.2 km (4½ miles), 30 m (100 ft) change in elevation, 3 hours

Begins at Grand Wash car park; ends at State 24. This is an old track formerly used by cattle, one of the five natural corridors providing a way through Capitol Reef. The trail runs on the level, following the dry bed of the wash, where delicate, fragrant flowers grow among the pebbles. On either side there are huge rock walls which at one point are barely 6 m (20 ft) apart. Grand Wash Trail also provides access to more demanding trails for experienced hikers, such as those that cross Shinob Canyon and Bear Canyon;

one path, in poor condition, which runs through Bear Canyon leads to the top of Fern's Nipple, 2,120 m (6,953 ft) high. (Before venturing into Bear Canyon it is advisable to consult a ranger.)

Cassidy Arch Trail   M

5.6 km (3½ miles), 270 m (885 ft) change in elevation, 3 hours

Begins at Grand Wash car park; ends at Cassidy Arch. The trail, once it has left the bottom of Grand Wash Canyon, ascends the high north wall (strenuous climb) which is made up of three different sandstone formations: Wingate, Kayenta and Navajo, the first two red, and the third, comprising the arch itself, creamy gold. Growing from rock fissures along the trail are nut (or piñon) pines and Utah junipers, two typical conifers of hot, arid climes, which assume strangely contorted shapes. The natural arch, invisible from below, takes its name from the famous bandit Butch Cassidy, who grew up at Circleville (west of the park) and often rode through Capitol Reef in the course of his eventful career. The trail is linked to the Cohab Canyon Trail and the Frying Pan Trail.

The irregular lines between the rock formations reveal how the strata formed incoherently at different periods. This geological phenomenon is clearly visible in the vertical walls of the reef.

Frying Pan Trail   M

4.8 km (3 miles) outward only, 180 m (590 ft) change in elevation, 1½ hours

Begins at Cassidy Arch Trail; ends at Cohab Canyon Trail. This trail, which can be covered equally well in either direction, links the Cohab Canyon and Cassidy Arch Trails, making up what is surely one of the most fascinating itineraries in the park. The path itself has a few strenuous climbs but is not at all difficult and is the only marked trail at the summit of the Waterpocket Fold. Short diversions lead to viewpoints which overlook the Scenic Drive.

Golden Throne Trail   M

6.4 km (4 miles), 330 m (1,082 ft) change in elevation, 4 hours

Begins at the Capitol Gorge car park; ends at the Golden Throne. A tiring climb leads up to the base of the Golden Throne, an enormous golden-yellow sandstone rock which dominates the surrounding country. Expert hikers can continue beyond the end of the marked trail and branch off to climb some of the less frequented peaks of Capitol Reef.

MORE DEMANDING TRAILS

The harsh, wild scenery and the vast distances make this park an ideal area for longer hikes and exploration treks. The zones most suitable for such activities are the northern desert and central-southern sectors, where countless itineraries can be planned. Many are well known and much frequented, some of them marked with mounds of stones, but others are seldom, if ever, visited. Information may be obtained from the Visitor Center, together with detailed maps of the zones concerned. It is essential to consult the rangers about necessary equipment and any difficulties that may be encountered along the way. The following are just a few of the routes that are possible, arranged according to zones.

NORTHERN SECTOR
Cathedral Valley – South Desert – Hartnet Desert

Access: Three off-trail tracks only. From the north, one path descends directly from the summit of

HOW TO PHOTOGRAPH CAPITOL GORGE

Marvellous photographs can be taken inside Capitol Gorge, but it is best to choose the central hours of the day; if the subject is a narrow gorge, the rock face may be completely in shadow at dawn or dusk so that no detail shows up. Interesting close-up pictures can be obtained of sections of the highly coloured rock forming the walls of the canyon, by using lenses of about 200 mm and taking vertical shots.

The Egyptian Temple was carved out by erosion, assuming the likeness in shape and structure of a temple of the pharaohs.

On page 206: The Golden Throne dates back to the Jurassic geological era, between 135 and 190 million years ago.

FLORA

In the park and neighbouring zones the plants form characteristic associations which depend principally on the availability of water and the type of rock on which they grow. The dry desert climate has a profound effect on the vegetation, composed for the most part of shrubby species well adapted to a scarcity of water. In the clays of the Mancos Formation, poor in nutritive elements, the few plants which do flourish include the saltbush (*Atriplex confertifolia*), a small bush of the family Chenopodiaceae, and curly mesquite grass (*Hilaria* sp.).

Plants that grow on the coloured Morrison clay, practically devoid of vegetation, include the milk vetch (*Astragalus* sp.) a typical leguminous plant recognizable by its thorny leaves, which tolerates high concentrations of selenium in the soil; this element, associated with the presence of uranium deposits, is poisonous to most plants. The soft sandstones of the Entrada Formation are notable for the Mormon tea (*Ephedra* spp.), which associates with clumps of salvia (*Salvia* sp.) and various grasses. At those points where the water level in the subsoil rises seasonally so as to be reached by plant roots, as for example in the dry bed of a wash, even a few trees manage to grow, such as the Fremont poplar (*Populus fremontii*), the Gambel oak (*Quercus gambelii*), the omnipresent clumps of sagebrush (*Artemisia*), pictured below, rabbitbrush (*Chrysothamnus*) and greasewood (*Sarcobatus vermiculatus*), unless they are all swept away by flood water.

The rock buttresses and deep canyons of the Waterpocket Fold are the kingdom of the nut (or piñon) pine (*Pinus edulis*) and the Utah juniper; associated with this pair of conifers, which manage to grow in rock clefts, are various shrubby plants which vary according to the rock formation.

At the southern tip of the park, where Hall's Creek Gorge descends to a height of just over 1,000 m (3,280 ft), blackbrush (*Coleogyne ramosissima*) grows. This is the most interesting section of the park from the botanical point of view: the side canyons of Hall's Creek contain varied and spectacular associations which, isolated from one another and confined to their own moist niches, constitute miniature jungles which include delicate ferns such as the Venus's hair (*Adiantum capillus-veneris*) and colourful flowers (orchids, monkey flowers, columbines, etc.). On the other hand, to the north, where the Waterpocket Fold ends and the flanks of Thousand Lake Mountain rise to a height of 2,600 m (8,530 ft), the landscape is dominated by woods of western yellow pine (*P. ponderosa*), and is notable for at least a hundred different species of alpine flowers which grow nowhere else in the park.

Two different ways in which water and wind erosion may occur can be seen on the rock walls most exposed to the elements inside Capitol Gorge, where it is possible to take easy and pleasant walks.

Thousand Lake Mountain; one begins at Caineville (42.8 km/26¾ miles), situated east of the park on State 24; and the third, 46.2 km (29 miles) long, branches off State 24 19.5 km (12¼ miles) east of the Visitor Center, running parallel to the margin of the South Desert.

Routes: You can follow the beds of many dry streams which furrow the southern slopes of Thousand Lake Mountain at the northern edge of the park, as well as Deep Creek and Water Canyon which cross the South Desert. All these routes are well away from roads and marked trails, in arid, unexplored, completely desert territory: they are extremely arduous and for expert trekkers only (D).

CENTRAL-SOUTHERN SECTOR

Access: By two dirt roads normally negotiable by ordinary cars. Notom Road, which flanks the western slope of the Waterpocket Fold for almost 80 km (50 miles), branches off State 24 at the eastern boundary of the park and descends southward in the direction of Bullfrog Marina; Burr Trail Road (58.4 km/36½ miles), an old cattle track, climbs the ridge of the Waterpocket Fold and reaches the town of Boulder on the Notom Road.

Routes: In this sector, too, most of the walks are along dry stream beds and inside canyons. An in-

formation board with a map is situated at the junction of Notom Road and Burr Trail Road. The distances, the lack of water and the intense heat make the majority of these treks very strenuous and for experts only (D).

Burro, Cottonwood, Fivemile and Sheets Washes   D

These are four small washes which are cut into the other rampart of the Waterpocket Fold in the stretch of about 16 km (10 miles) between Pleasant Creek to the north and Oak Creek to the south. All four make excellent one-day trips, starting from Notom Road, which crosses them. The scenery is marvellous, with high rock walls, gorges and pools of water, which teem with life and reflect the colours of the rocks above.

Red Canyon   E

6.4 km (4 miles), 2½ hours

Begins and ends at the Cedar Mesa campground. A simple walk that features an enormous canyon.

Upper Muley Trail Canyon   D

12.5/15.5 km (7¾/9¾ miles) outward only

Begins at the Burr Trail Road and ends at Bitter Creek Divide. The first stretch of this route (4.8 km/3 miles), through narrow gorges and numerous arches, can also be covered in off-road vehicles and will lead to the Strike Valley Overlook, a viewpoint over the Waterpocket Fold. From where the dirt road ends, continue on foot for 7.7 km (4¾ miles), through The Narrows, to the junction with the Rim Route Trail. Here there are three options: to return to the departure point by retracing your steps; to follow the Rim Route Trail which climbs outside the canyon and skirts the left rim to reach the Burr Trail Road; or to continue for another 3 km (2 miles) to the end of the canyon, this last option being the most difficult.

Lower Muley Twist Canyon   D

27.3 km (17 miles), 2 days

Begins at the Burr Trail Road, about 3 km (2 miles) east of the crossing with Notom Road; ends at The

---

THE ANASAZI CULTURE

Not far from Capitol Reef National Park, towards the east, is Anasazi State Park. The entrance is near the town of Boulder, 64 km (40 miles) south of Torrey on State Highway 12, and it can also be reached by the Burr Trail Road. In this park you can see archaeological excavations and ruins of the home of the Anasazi Indians from about 1,000 years ago, a people which left the first signs of its culture on American territory around 750 B.C. The Anasazi built pit dwellings, at first fairly rudimentary and close to the surface, but in due course much deeper and with simple but effective systems for letting out smoke. About A.D. 500 the Anasazi began to live in walled buildings above ground level, packed one against the other in rock faces or on stretches of rocky ground. The biggest and most astonishing complex is Cliff Palace, comprising 200 rooms and twenty-three kivas, areas reserved for ceremonial purposes and used only by the men of the tribe. Around the fourteenth century the Anasazi tradition began to retreat under the pressure of new Indian tribes, perhaps Navajos and Apaches, and very soon the entire Indian population of the southwest was subjugated by powerful armies from overseas as the great Spanish invasion got under way.

FAUNA

In spite of the harsh environmental conditions, the fauna of Capitol Reef is rich and varied. Some animals have a wide distribution and migrate long distances; these are mostly predators and scavengers, such as the bay lynx (*Lynx rufus*), the grey fox (*Urocyon cinereoargenteus*), the raven (*Corvus corax*), the golden eagle (*Aquila chrysaetos*) and the puma (*Felis concolor*).

The majority of animals, nevertheless, prefer to remain in a specific habitat. The kangaroo rat (*Dipodomys* spp.) and the American badger (*Taxidea taxus*) dig burrows in the sand, sheltered by clumps of desert shrubs, the piñon jay (*Gymnorhinus cyanocephalus*) settles on the branches of pines, feeding on cones, and the canyon frog (*Hyla arenicolor*) never strays far from pools in the higher reaches of the Fold.

One mammal which is perfectly adapted to the canyon environment is the ringtail cat (*Bassariscus astutus*). This relative of the raccoon has a long tail of black and white rings and hunts around pools at night for rodents. Thanks to its remarkable agility, it can dart rapidly along ledges and into narrow clefts in the vertical rock walls, seldom returning without prey. Another mammal commonly found in the park is the white-tailed prairie dog (*Cynomys gunnisoni*), recently reintroduced into the northern sector of the park having been brought to the brink of extinction by hunting and the destruction of its natural habitat. Today the colonies of these attractive animals are strictly protected.

As in other American parks, the mule deer (*Odocoileus hemionus*), pictured below, is widely distributed.

Post, some 5 km (3 miles) south of this junction. Lower Muley Twist Canyon is the road used by the first pioneers who travelled from Escalante to Hall's Crossing on the Colorado, around 1880. The canyon is hewn out by the waters of an abnormal wash which, instead of cutting across the Waterpocket Fold, runs in a north-south direction to the confluence with Hall's Creek. It derives its name from those same pioneers who described how the rock walls clustered so closely together that they forced the mules to twist their way through like snakes. Just over 6 km (3¾ miles) from the mouth of the canyon, there is a short-cut of about 3 km (2 miles) which branches off to the left, leading over the ridge of the Waterpocket Fold to The Post, an old cowboy camp alongside the Notom Road. This short-cut should be chosen by anyone wishing to cover the entire route in a single day. Alternatively, you can continue south for another 12.8 km (8 miles) as far as Hall's Creek, where the Muley Twist Canyon ends. From here the return journey starts: the track bends north and after 8 km (5 miles) crosses a broad, dry valley covered with shrubs, leading to The Post.

The Castle columns, clearly visible from State Highway 24, are composed of the sandstone of the Wingate Formation; their red colour is unmistakable because they are quite separate from the cream-coloured domes and towers of the Navajo Formation.

INDEX